Illinois Central Railroad Company

A Guide to the Illinois Central Railroad Lands

Illinois Central Railroad Company

A Guide to the Illinois Central Railroad Lands

ISBN/EAN: 9783337840051

Printed in Europe, USA, Canada, Australia, Japan

Cover: Foto ©Andreas Hilbeck / pixelio.de

More available books at **www.hansebooks.com**

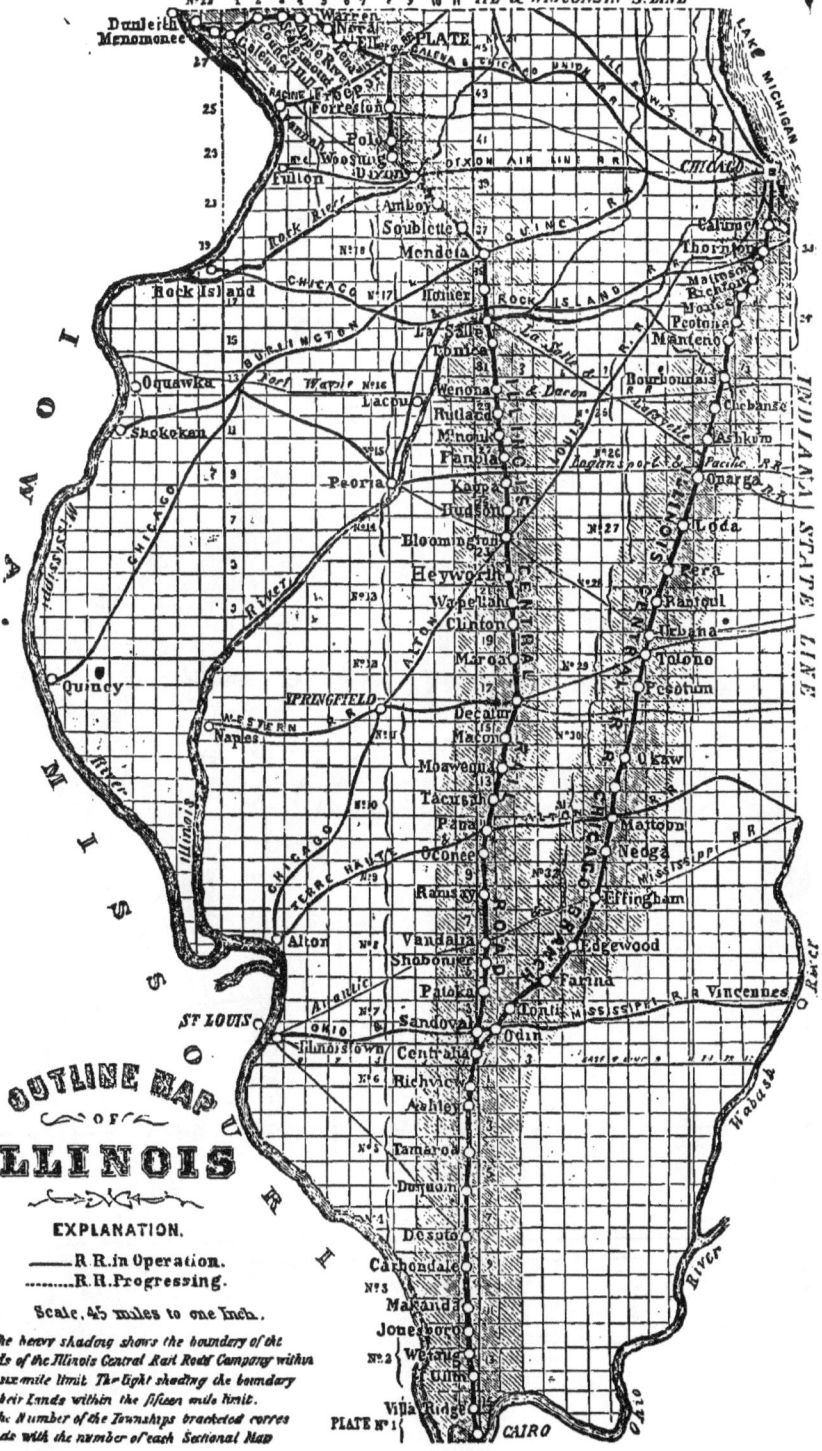

OUTLINE MAP OF ILLINOIS

EXPLANATION.

——— R.R. in Operation.
········· R.R. Progressing.

Scale, 45 miles to one Inch.

The heavy shading shows the boundary of the lands of the Illinois Central Rail Road Company within the six mile limit. The light shading the boundary of their Lands within the fifteen mile limit.

The Number of the Townships bracketed corresponds with the number of each Sectional Map.

ILL. & WISCONSIN S. LINE

LAKE MICHIGAN

INDIANA STATE LINE

MISSOURI

IOWA

Dunleith
Menomonee
Forreston
Polo
Woosung
Fulton
Dixon
Amboy
Soublette
Mendota
Rock Island
Homer
La Salle
Tonica
Oquawka
Lacon
Wenona
Rutland
Shokokon
Minonk
Panola
Peoria
Kappa
Hudson
Bloomington
Heyworth
Wapella
Clinton
Maroa
Quincy
SPRINGFIELD
Naples
Decatur
Macon
Moawequa
Tacusa
Pana
Oconee
Ramsay
Alton
Vandalia
Shobonier
Patoka
Sandoval
ST. LOUIS
Illinstown
Centralia
Richview
Ashley
Tamaroa
Duquoin
Desoto
Carbondale
Makanda
Jonesboro
Wetaug
Ullin
Villa Ridge
CAIRO

CHICAGO
Calume
Thornton
Matteson
Richton
Monee
Peotone
Manteno
Bourbonnais
Chebanse
Ashkum
Onarga
Loda
Pera
Rantoul
Urbana
Tolono
Pesotum
Okaw
Mattoon
Neoga
Effingham
Edgewood
Farina
Odin
Vincennes

PLATE No. 1

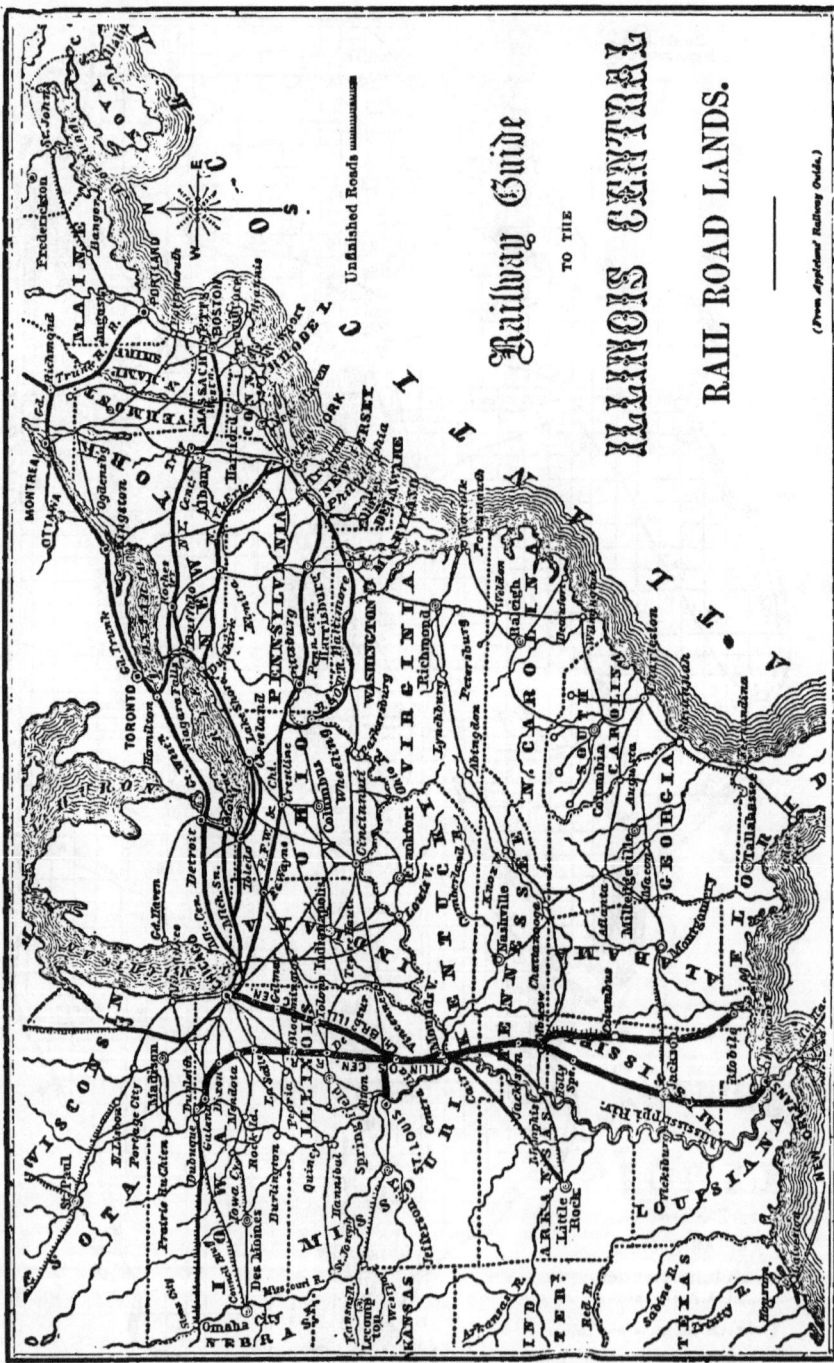

Railway Guide

TO THE

ILLINOIS CENTRAL

RAIL ROAD LANDS.

(From Appletons' Railway Guide.)

Unfinished Roads ....

PRAIRIE SCENE IN ILLINOIS.

A GUIDE

TO THE

ILLINOIS CENTRAL

Railroad Lands.

THE

ILLINOIS CENTRAL RAILROAD COMPANY,

OFFER FOR SALE

OVER 1,400,000 ACRES

OF SELECTED

Prairie and Wood Lands,

In Tracts of forty acres and upwards, suitable for Farms, on long credits and low prices, situated on each side of their Railroad, extending through the State of Illinois.

CHICAGO:
ILLINOIS CENTRAL RAILROAD OFFICE.
1861.

NOTE.

It has been found impossible to answer the numerous letters that are daily received, in reference to these lands. To such, this Pamphlet will be sent in reply to the questions asked.

SECTIONAL MAPS of the Lands of the Company, showing the precise position of every piece of land in the State, owned by the Company, can be had at the Land Department, by remitting fifty cents in postage stamps. Plats of their towns, at the various stations throughout the State, can also be seen.

For any further information, apply personally or by letter, in English, French, or German, to

J. M. REDMOND,
Acting Commissioner.

THE STATE OF ILLINOIS.

ITS AREA AND EXTENT.

THE greatest extent of Illinois is on the meridian of Cairo, being 378 miles. Its average width is about 150 miles;—the greatest width being 210 miles, near the latitude of Urbana. It lies between latitude 37° and 42½° North, and longitude 10° 5' and 14° West of Washington.

The area of the State is 55,409 square miles. Some of the States contain a larger area, but that area is made up of mountainous or sterile tracts, which must forever remain sparsely inhabited; whereas Illinois presents a nearly uniform fertility of soil throughout its entire extent. To compare it with other States, Illinois is nearly as large as the six New England States put together, and it is safe to say that its agricultural resources are twice as great as the whole of them. It has nearly 10,000 more square miles than the State of New York;

is larger than Pennsylvania and New Jersey together; and is nearly eight times as large as Massachusetts. It is larger than England by 5,000 square miles, and nearly half as large as the entire kingdom of Great Britain; and with its resources as well developed, could sustain a population of 15,000,000. It is more than twice as large as Belgium and Holland together, and nearly one-fourth as large as the entire Empire of Austria.

The grant of land to the Illinois Central Railroad Company embraces 4,055 square miles,—very nearly as large an area as that comprised within the State of Connecticut, twice as large as Delaware, more than half as large as Massachusetts, about the same size as the Electorate of Hesse-Cassel, three-fourths as large as the Grand Duchy of Baden, and half as large as the Grand Duchy of Tuscany.

Illinois must always occupy a commanding position in the union of States, forming as she does the water-shed between the valley of the Mississippi and that of the St. Lawrence. In the intercourse and traffic, thus far but imperfectly developed, between these two great valleys, THE ILLINOIS CENTRAL RAILROAD must be regarded as a most important part of the great thoroughfare which is now opened to the Gulf of Mexico, by which Chicago is made as accessible to New Orleans and Mobile, as she is to Boston, New York, and Philadelphia.

COMMERCIAL FACILITIES.

The means of intercommunication provided by nature are unsurpassed. The State is bounded on the West and South by two great navigable rivers, and for fifty miles on the Northeast by Lake Michigan; while the interior is penetrated for more than two hundred miles by the Illinois river, whose waters are connected with the lake by the Illinois and Michigan Canal. About two-thirds of the boundaries of the State is made up of navigable rivers, amounting to about 1,000 miles in length.

The artificial communications are not less complete. Within less than ten years, there have been constructed 2,682 miles of railway, at a cost of $96,284,445, by which, with one or two exceptions, every county seat is brought within fifteen miles of some great thoroughfare. The population has increased from 477,000 in 1840, to 855,384 in 1850, to 1,300,251 in 1855, and to probably 1,700,000 in 1859. Illinois is now the fourth State in the Union in numerical force.

FACE OF THE COUNTRY.

The profile of the country, adjacent to THE ILLINOIS CENTRAL RAILROAD, does not present one uniform dead level, but a succession of gentle undulations and depressions which have been not inaptly compared to the swells of the ocean. The culminating points, which are in the northwestern part of the State, attain an elevation of about 800 feet above the Ohio river at Cairo, and about 400 feet above the level of Lake Michigan. The valleys are valleys of denudation, cutting through the superficial deposits, and occasionally exposing the rocky strata beneath; while from the main channels start numerous ravines, like the intervals between the fingers when the hand is extended. These are everywhere bordered with timber, and occasional isolated clumps are seen, known in the language of the country as groves; while the plains are clothed with a luxuriant growth of prairie grass. The Chicago branch, 250 miles in length, runs through the Grand Prairie, which, with the exception of occasional groves, presents an almost interminable plain, of which the natural product is prairie-grass. Here the similitude of the ocean becomes more striking. The timber belts resemble wooded shores, while the clumps may be likened to islands rising up from a wide expanse of waving green.

The surface is covered with superficial materials consisting of yellow loam, blue clay, the latter always subordinate, sand and pebbles, rudely stratified, with occasional boulders of granite, upon which reposes a rich vegetable mould from eighteen inches to two feet thick, constituting an almost inexhaustible supply of nutriment for crops, for all time.

The swales, or sloughs (provincially *slues*), as well as the more level portions of the prairie, contain a dark sandy soil, intermixed with much organic matter; while along the streams and ravines the soil is a light yellow loam. These distinctive differences are well understood by every settler, and the term "prairie soil" to him conveys a precise meaning. It is a popular but mistaken belief that this region was once densely covered with trees, and that their disappearance is to be ascribed to the annual fires that swept over it, long before it became known to the whites, consuming every form of vegetation, except where it was protected by the streams and ravines. There is no evidence that, in the previous physical history of this region, the arborescent vegetation was more extended than it is now. The prairies result from the character of the soil, and their origin is no more of a mystery than that of the steppes of Northern Asia, the pampas of Brazil, or the llanos of Venezuela. In the rich black mould of the plains the prairie-grass finds its appropriate nourishment to the exclusion of other forms of vegetation; but this in its turn is supplanted by many of the tame grasses. On the other hand, the yellow soil along the ravines and alluvial bottoms gives sustenance to a growth of trees, the commonest of which are burr, jack and white oak, hickory, black walnut, linden, poplar, and honey locust. As we proceed south, to the region below the Terre Haute and Alton Railroad, the groves begin to encroach upon the prairies until finally the whole region becomes densely wooded. Below Carbondale, the country is covered with a primeval forest, except where the axe of the settler has leveled it to the ground.

The changes in the soil are not less marked. Passing from the rich black mould of Urbana, as we approach

Effingham, the soil begins to assume a greyish tint, and thence by imperceptible gradations, passes into a light yellow or reddish loam. These soils produce the finest varieties of winter wheat, and those scourges of other regions—the weevil and the blight—are comparatively unknown.

CLASSIFICATION OF SOILS.

There are well-marked differences in the soils of the Illinois Central Railroad Lands.

1⁰. *Black Prairie Soil,*—consisting of a dark-colored, friable mould, often two feet deep, and containing a large amount of organic matter, intermixed with potash derived from the annual burnings of the prairie-grass, from time immemorial. The substratum is a mixture of clay and gravel, well calculated to retain moisture; but not so much so as to cause it to bake when exposed to the sun, or to render the surface soil cold and wet. The prairie soil makes first-class corn lands, and is so rich in organic matter that it may be cropped for years without showing any signs of exhaustion. Spring wheat, barley, oats, potatoes, and the domestic grasses, here find appropriate food. The prairies afford admirable grazing farms, and there are farmers who fatten yearly more than a thousand head of cattle.

The sloughs, when drained and sowed with grasses, will make the finest meadow lands known, far surpassing the uplands in fertility.

This kind of soil largely predominates on the Chicago Branch, as well as on the Main Line, in the central portion of the State.

2⁰. *Grey Prairie Soil.*—Between Nioga and Effingham on the Branch, and below Pana, on the Main Line, we notice a change in the soil, the black mould giving place to a grey soil, which, though not so prolific in Indian corn, produces excellent crops of winter wheat, and is a superior fruit-growing region. The lines between the two classes of soil are not well marked, but there is a gradual blending along the borders. The prairies become smaller in extent, and the groves more numerous. This soil is susceptible of a fine mechanical division, and by many is esteemed quite as highly as the black mould of the more northerly prairies.

3°. *Wood Soil.*—This soil, which predominates in the southern part of the State, consists of a fine yellowish, or reddish loam, or a mixture of sand and clay, in about the proportions to form brick, and is sufficiently porous to enable the water to leach through, and the rootlets of trees to penetrate it. It does not bake when exposed to the heats of summer, or form a water-bearing stratum during the rains of spring and fall. It is not unusual to find this soil covered with hazel brush, which is the precursor of the hickory, gum, oak, linden, etc., etc. This soil is well adapted to the culture of winter, or flint wheat, and the choicest varieties are produced. The harvest comes off as early as the tenth of June, and by July or August, it is ready for market. The market value of this wheat is 12 to 15 cents above the ordinary varieties, and it is sought for by millers from New York, St. Louis and Ohio. It was not until the opening of the Illinois Central Railroad that wheat was cultivated to any considerable extent; it now forms the great staple of the region, and has been the means of conferring upon the farmer, uncounted wealth. Their experience has been that winter-wheat is a sure and remunerative crop. Samples of white winter-wheat from the counties of Union, Perry and Pulaski are now in the Land Department. The berry is large and plump, and weighs upwards of 60 lbs. to the bushel, and the yield was more than 40 bushels to the acre.

This soil is the natural habitat for the apple, peach, pear, plum and grape, and the culture of these fruits is rapidly extending. Near Makanda, Jonesboro', and Cobden, there are thousands of acres devoted to the cultivation of peaches. The apples produced are large, fair and plump; and look very differently from their eastern relations.

Mr. C. T. Chase, a practical horticulturalist, in a work*
recently published, thus speaks of this region:

"Much of the soil of Southern Illinois is also admirably adapted to
fruit. Such is the texture in many locations that drainage is of less
importance than in the North. The heavily timbered lands of that
section, including a series of elevated ridges extending entirely across
the State, and into the adjoining States, combine essential qualifications
of soil, climate, elevation and exposure, that fit them in an eminent
degree for successful fruit-culture. In these regions, the highest knobs
are at present preferred. As the timber is cleared away, the frost
lines will probably follow down the hill-sides, and many fine situations
for fruit will be developed which are now unfit. The indications point
to a time, at no distant period, when by judicious culture, Southern
Illinois and a part of Missouri will become the fruit-garden of the West."

4°. *Alluvial Soil.*—The immediate valley of the Mississippi consists of a wide belt of level land, occasionally
subject to overflow, known as "The American Bottom."
The soil is a highly comminuted loam, rich in organic
matter, the result of successive depositions of the river.
It has all of the fertility of that of the Nile, and is well
adapted to the growth of Indian corn, broom corn, sor-
ghum, tobacco, hemp, and all those crops which are supposed to exhaust its fertility. Cotton was formerly grown
here, and as far north even, as Sangamon county, in sufficient quantities for all domestic purposes; and there is no
apparent reason why its culture might not be successfully
resumed.

COMPOSITION OF SOILS.

In many parts of the world, it is found necessary to improve the soil by mixing and combining different earths;
and also, by adding to the organic matter. But Nature,
so far as relates to the soils of Illinois, has kindly per-
formed these offices for man. Experience has shown that
a soil, composed of one earth alone, whether it be sand,
clay, or lime, is unproductive; but that the best soil consists of a due admixture of all these earths.

In examining the mechanical texture of the soils of Illinois, we find that the proportion of clay varies from 18 to

---

*The Prairie Fruit Culturalist.

64 per-cent.; of sand, from 25 to 75 per-cent.; and of lime, from 1.3 to 3.3 per-cent.; but what is most note-worthy with regard to them, is the remarkably fine state of subdivision in the particles. The soil, when dried and crushed, crumbles into an almost impalpable powder, and hence is in the best condition to afford nutriment to plants.

Most soils, too, require the addition of organized matter, or manures, to preserve their fertility. In England, and in the Atlantic States, this annual application of manures often costs more per acre, than the fee of the Illinois lands. The mechanical analysis of these soils shows that there is present from 5 to 10 per-cent. of organic matter; while the chemical analysis indicates from .18 to .33 per-cent. of nitrogen. It would take a half century of cropping to exhaust this accumulation of organic matter.

Mr. James Caird, M. P., the Times Commissioner of Agriculture, and the highest agricultural authority in England, in the fall of 1858, passed over the lands adjacent to the Illinois Central Railroad, and after speaking of the inexhaustible fertility of the soil, he proceeds to add:

"Its chemical composition has been ascertained for me by Professor Voelcker, consulting chemist to the Royal Agricultural Society of England, to whom I sent four samples of prairie soil for analysis, brought by me from different and distant points of the lands belonging to the Illinois Central Railway Company. They bear out completely the high character for fertility which practice and experience had already proved these soils to possess. The most noticeable feature in the analysis, as it appears to me, is the very large quantity of nitrogen which each of these soils contains, nearly twice as much as the most fertile soils of Britain. In each case, taking the soil at an average depth of ten inches, an acre of these prairies will contain upwards of three tons of nitrogen, and as a heavy crop of wheat with its straw contains about fifty-two pounds of nitrogen, there is thus a natural store of ammonia in this soil sufficient for more than a hundred wheat crops. In Dr. Voelcker's words, 'it is the large amount of nitrogen, and the beautiful state of division, that impart a peculiar character to these soils, and distinguish them so favorably.' They are soils upon which flax, I imagine, could be grown in perfection, supposing the climate to be otherwise favorable. *I have never before analyzed soils which contained so much nitrogen, nor do I find any record of soils richer in nitrogen than these.*"—*Prairie Farming,. pp.* 77, 78. *Lond. Ed.*

COMPOSITION OF PRAIRIE AND OTHER FERTILE SOILS.

	Prairie Soils from Illinois Central Railway Lands, Analyzed by Professor Voelcker, Consulting Chemist of the Royal Agricultural Society of England.				Soil from Old Red Sandstone of England.	Wheat Soils from Scotland. Analyzed by Professor Anderson, Chemist to the Highland Agricultural Society of Scotland.			
	No. 1.	No. 2.	No. 3.	No. 4.		and Lothian.	East Lothian.	Perthshire.	Berwickshire.
Org. Matter & Water of Com.	7.54	5.76	9.77	9.06	4.38	10.19	6.82	8.55	6.67
Alumina,	6.67	6.55	8.58	8.74	4.51	6.93	5.54	14.04	7.36
Oxides of Iron,	4.96	2.57	4.13	4.30	3.15	5.17	4.41	4.87	4.32
Lime,	1.37	.35	1.64	1.13	.77	1.22	1.39	0.83	2.70
Magnesia,	1.03	1.63	.82	.61	.63	1.08	0.74	1.02	1.63
Potash,	1.69	1.40	1.20	1.29	.74	0.35	1.71	2.80	0.55
Soda,	.82	.58	.83	.50	.22	0.43	0.67	1.43	0.36
Phosphoric Acid,	.08	.65	.12	.10	.12	0.43	0.14	0.24	0.22
Sulphuric Acid,	.07	.06	.14	.08	.06	0.04	0.10	0.09	0.06
Silica,	76.04	80.68	71.75	74.11	85.11	71.55	74.39	63.19	78.52
Water,						2.58	4.43	2.70	2.50
Carbonic Acid and Loss,	.74	.53	.82	.09	.31	.3	.17	0.05	.12
	1:0.00	100.00	100.00	100.00	100.00	100.00	100.00	100.00	100.00
Containing Nitrogen, Equal to Ammonia,	.30 / .36	.25 / .31	.33 / .40	.34 / .41	.18 / .22	.23	.18	.21	.14
MECHANICAL ANALYSIS.									
Clay,	64.14	46.76	58.90	62.76	18.09				
Lime,	1.37	3.35	1.84	1.13	1.37				
Sand,	26.95	47.13	29.49	27.07	76.16				
Organic Matter,	7.54	6.76	9.77	9.05	4.38				
	100.00	100.00	100.00	100.00	100.00				

AREA OF CULTIVABLE LAND.

It is supposed by many, who have not investigated the climatology of the West, that the rich prairies, like those of Illinois, continue to the base of the Rocky Mountains. The really desirable lands lie east of longitude 95°, and embrace Illinois, the Eastern and Southern portions of Iowa, the Eastern portion of Kansas, and Southern Minnesota and Southern Wisconsin. They have already passed out of the possession of the General Government. After having crossed the Missouri river, we enter upon a series of plains, whose prevailing vegetation is the artemisia and the buffalo grass—types characteristic of an arid climate. Almost the only form of arborescent vegetation is the cotton-wood, which is restricted to the immediate valleys of the streams. From the conditions of climate, this vast region, embracing at least 25° of longitude, must forever remain sparsely inhabited.

"The most marked single feature" (says Blodgett, in his Climatology of the United States, p. 155) "is the absence of atmospheric moisture, or the low measure of humidity, when rain is not absolutely falling. This arid character begins to be felt at the 95th meridian, and at the 98th or 100th, it causes an abrupt contrast with the country east."

Starting from the 95th degree, the rains diminish rapidly as we proceed westward, until, before reaching the Rocky Mountains, they disappear almost altogether. This dryness of the atmosphere gives rise to a variety of climatic conditions, which are unobserved to the eastward : abrupt transitions in the temperature, the thermometer rising to 75° or 80° at mid-day, and falling below the freezing point at night, or before sunrise. These sudden changes are fatal to the growth of all those plants, of which Indian corn is the type.

If we consult the rain-charts, which have been constructed from the observations of the officers at the various military posts, and from those of scientific explorers, we shall find that, while the mean distribution of rain for the year in Illinois is 42 inches in the northern, and 45 inches in the southern part of the State, the gradations, as we proceed west, are rapid to 35, 30, 25, 20, 15 and 10. The belt where the annual fall is intermediate between 40 and 30 inches, is less than 50 miles wide. It may be safely assumed that, for successful agriculture, the annual fall of rain should amount to 35 inches, and inside of this limit is comprised the great grain-growing region of the United States. If we trace this line upon the map, we shall find that it is subject to abrupt curvatures. Starting at Chicago, it bears northwesterly to Fort Winnebago, then sweeps round and crosses the Mississippi, near the north boundary of Iowa; then trends southwesterly, a hundred miles east of Fort Des Moines and Fort Leavenworth, and thence is protracted into Texas.

We thus see that there are physical conditions which interpose an effectual barrier to the progress of settlement to the westward. Emigration has already reached the line where it must pause. It needs no prophetic vision to predict the time, and that not far distant, when every rood of desirable land in Illinois will be appropriated and improved.

THE ILLINOIS CENTRAL RAILROAD.

This is the longest continuous line of road, under the control of a single corporation, in the United States,—the entire length being 706 miles. It traverses the whole State, from north to south, intersecting, in its course, every railway in the State. It starts from Cairo, at the junction of the Ohio and Mississippi rivers, and pursues a course nearly north 111 miles to Centralia; at a point four miles north, the road branches—the one pursuing a northeasterly course to Chicago, 250 miles distant; while the other pursues a northerly course to Mendota, and thence bears northwesterly to Galena and Dunleith on the Mississippi river, opposite Dubuque :—the distance between the northern and southern terminus being 454 miles.

This road traverses nearly 6° of latitude (from 37° N. to 42½° N.), embracing the most favored portion of the northern temperate zone. Above this belt, the season is not long enough to raise the most profitable varieties of corn; below it, the climate is warm enough to grow cotton. Thus it is midway between the biting frosts of the North and the sultry heats of the South. The moisture is so equally diffused, that, however unpropitious the season, there is always a surplus of the great staples grown. The variation of climate between Galena and Cairo is as great as between Boston and Richmond. Migration usually follows lines of latitude. Illinois will, therefore, continue to receive the tide of population from the overcrowded districts of the Old and New World, until her immense capacity for occupation and expansion is fully tested.

The main line of the road has been in operation four years, and the branches less than three. There is already a population of 500,000 adjacent thereto, and at intervals of not greater than ten miles, there are flourishing villages, some of which contain from 4,000 to 15 000 inhabi-

tants. Churches have been planted, and school districts organized, so that the benefits of religious and intellectual culture are provided for all.

Table (A), appended to this Pamphlet, will exhibit at a glance the progress of settlement since the opening of this line.

The road is built in a substantial manner, and is equipped with superior locomotives and cars. Two passenger trains pass over the line each way daily, while the freight trains have a passenger car attached. Commodious passenger and freight houses have been erected at nearly every station, and there is a telegraphic line coterminous with the road, by which the farmer is daily advised of the state of the markets.

ILLINOIS CENTRAL RAILROAD LANDS.

These lands were granted by the General Government to the State, in aid of the construction of a railroad from Chicago to Cairo, and from Cairo to Dunleith; and by the State were transferred to the Central Railroad Company upon certain conditions, which have been fully complied with. The grant comprised every alternate section* of even numbers, for six sections in width on each side of the road and branches, and in case of deficiency, by reason of sale or preëmption, the agent of the State was

---

*Note.—To those who are unacquainted with the system of the Government surveys of the public lands, it would be well to state that the territory is laid out by rectilinear lines, into towns, ranges, and sections, and these sections are subdivided into eighths. A township embraces thirty-six sections, and is six miles square, or includes thirty-six square miles. A section is one mile square, 640 acres, and is subdivided into halves, 320 acres; quarters, 160 acres; and eighths, 40 acres, which is the lowest Government subdivision. The ranges are laid off East and West from a principal meridian, running due North and South, and the townships are laid off North and South from a base line running due East and West. In a timber-region, the section corners are blazed on the trees; but in a prairie-region, they are indicated by mounds containing charcoal, into which a stake is driven. Thus, ordinarily, the bounds of every forty-acre tract are well defined. In numbering sections, you commence in the northeast corner of a township, and proceed from right to left, along the first tier, and from left to right through the second tier, and so on.

authorized to select an equal amount from alternate sections of Government land, within fifteen miles of the road.

The grant thus bestowed was - - -	2,595,000 acres.
Of which there have been appropriated to secure the payment of $17,-000,000 of Construction bonds,	2,000,000 acres.
To secure the payment of interest on said bonds, - - -	250,000 acres.
To secure the payment of $3,000,000 of Free-land bonds, - -	345,000 acres.

2,595,000 acres.

Hence, the Company's lands are respectively designated as CONSTRUCTION, FREE-LANDS, and INTEREST LANDS.

The Indenture with the Trustees prescribes that there shall be set apart,—

50,000 at	$20	per acre, until there be realized	$1,000,000.
350,000 at	15	"	"	"	5,200,000.
1,300,000 at	8	"	"	"	10,400,000.
300,000 at	5	"	"	"	1,500,000.

The Company have already sold about 1,200,000 acres of land, comprised in this grant, for the sum of $15,600,-000; this is less than one-half of the grant, and the unsold portion will undoubtedly bring a sum equal to that of the portion sold.

PRICES AND TERMS OF PAYMENT.

These vary according to location, quality, distance from stations, villages, &c., &c.

Lands immediately adjoining town sites, or in proximity to the road, are, of course, held at higher prices, and on somewhat shorter credits; but the *best farming lands*, in the most desirable localities, can be purchased at from $6 to $25 per acre.

The terms of sale for the bulk of these lands will be one year's interest in advance, at six per cent, per annum; and six interest notes at six per cent, payable respectively in one, two, three, four, five, and six years from date of sale; and four notes for principal, payable in four, five, six, and seven years from date of sale; the contract stipulating that one-tenth of the tract purchased shall be fenced and cultivated, *each and every year*, for five years from the date of sale, so that at the end of five years, one-half shall be fenced and under cultivation.

Twenty per cent. will be deducted from the valuation for cash, except the same should be at six dollars per acre, when the cash price will be five dollars per acre.

A purchaser's account would stand as follows, supposing he contracted for eighty acres of land at $10 per acre, on March 1, 1859.

		PRINCIPAL NOTES.	INTEREST NOTES.	TOTALS.
March 1, 1859, Cash Payment, 1 year's interest in advance, at 6 per cent.				$ 48 00
"	1860,		$48 00	48 00
"	1861,		- 48 00	48 00
"	1862,		- 48 00	48 00
"	1863,	$200 00	- 36 00	236 00
"	1864,	200 00	- 24 00	224 00
"	1865,	200 00	- 12 00	212 00
"	1866,	200 00		200 00

Upon these terms about 1,100,000 acres are offered for sale.

It is believed that the low price and long credit charged for these lands will enable a man of small capital, and with due industry, in ordinary seasons, to meet the payments as they become due, from the products of the soil; while the rapid settlement and development of the country will greatly enhance their value.

Certain tracts immediately adjoining stations, or for other causes specially valuable, are offered upon "Canal Terms;"—the terms are:

The payment of one-quarter cash, and interest on the balance for one year in advance, at six per cent. per annum, and three notes for the principal payable in one, two, and three years from the date of the agreement, with interest at six per cent. per annum in advance, added to the first and second.

Ten per cent. will be deducted from the valuation for full cash payment.

A purchaser's account would stand as follows, supposing he contracted for 80 acres of land at $10 per acre, on March 1st, 1859:

March 1, 1859, Cash Payment, ⅓ principal $200, and interest
on balance, 1 year at 6 per cent., $36, $236 00
"   1860,   "   "   "   "   224 00
"   1861,   "   "   "   "   212 00
"   1862, Cash Payment, ⅓ principal,   -   -   - 200 00

Upon these terms about 85,000 acres are offered for sale, no improvement clause being inserted in the contracts.

Town Lots, when the amount of sale is fifty dollars, or less, will be sold for one-half cash, and interest on the balance for one year in advance, at six per cent. per annum; the other one-half of principal payable in one year from the date of agreement. When the amount of sale is more than fifty dollars, the terms of sale will be one-third cash, and interest on the balance for one year in advance at six per cent. per annum; the remainder of the principal being payable in one and two years, with interest for one year in advance at six per cent. added to the first note.

Ten per cent. will be deducted from the valuation for full cash payment.

A deduction in the price of lots will be made to parties purchasing with an agreement to improve within six months from date of sale.

The Company own lots at most of the villages along their line. These villages are rapidly increasing in population, and offer good inducements to persons engaged in mercantile or professional pursuits, to settle therein. The Company have also valuable tracts of iron, coal, and timber-lands for sale.

MINERAL RESOURCES.

Although the greater portion of the country contiguous to the Illinois Central Railroad consists of rich undulating prairie, yet at various points the streams have cut through the superficial deposits, and laid bare the subjacent rocks, revealing and rendering accessible those materials, so useful to our comforts and conveniences.

The Illinois Central Railroad passes over all of those systems of rock, which are included between the Lower Silurian and the Upper Carboniferous. For more than two-thirds of the distance, the underlying rocks consist of shales, sandstones, and limestones, belonging to the Coal-Measures. Whether they constitute an unbroken assemblage of strata, dipping towards a common centre, or, like the Appalachian coal-field, are arranged in a series of corrugations, is a problem yet to be solved.

Coal.—This important combustible will be found so widely distributed throughout the prairie region of Illinois, that the absence of densely wooded tracts will subject the settler to no serious inconvenience. The Illinois Central Railroad Company, with an ample supply of wood at their command, at a cost not exceeding $2.50 per cord, are substituting, as a matter of economy, and convenience, coal-burning, in place of wood-burning, locomotives on their road, and other railroad companies are following their example.

There are three points from which the settlers can for

all time derive their supplies of fossil fuel, at an inconsiderable expense. At Duquoin, on the Illinois Central Railroad, 76 miles above Cairo, there is a seam of coal nearly 7 feet in thickness, which is worked by a shaft 70 feet deep. It possesses all of the qualities of a first class coal—freedom from sulphur, cleanliness when employed as a domestic fuel, and firmness to bear transportation.

At Danville, or rather Bryant, 36 miles east of Tolono, on the Great Western Railroad, a seam 6 feet thick is worked by a drift. It is a strong and valuable coal, and yields more than one-half of its weight in fixed carbon. The greater portion of the product of this mine is distributed over the Chicago branch.

At La Salle, on the Main line, there are three seams of coal, which average about four feet each in thickness, and all of which are embraced in a vertical range of about 225 feet. The workings here are more extensive than at any other point. The coal is of a fair quality, and besides the local consumption, some of it is sent to Dunleith and Chicago.

By inspecting the map it will be seen that, if from these three centres of supply we inscribe circles, with radii 150 miles in length, it will sweep every station on the line of the railroad. The cost of coal per ton, at the mouth of the pit is from $1 25 to $1 50 per ton; and the cost of transportation from 1 cent to 1¾ cents per ton per mile; consequently, coal can be sold at any station on the line at say $4 00 per ton. Twelve bushels, or one-half a ton of coal, are equivalent to a cord of wood. The cost of cutting a cord of wood four feet in length is about $1 00, and another dollar must be expended in cutting it stove length. It is therefore as cheap to buy coal as to cut wood for fuel, from one's own premises. The expense of fuel for a family in ordinary circumstances, on the prairie, need not exceed $30 per annum. A proper coal-stove for cooking can be found at any of the hardware shops.

Comparison between the Coals of the Illinois Coal-Field, and those of the Appalachian Coal-Field, brought to the Chicago Market.

Designation.	Distance from Chicago.	Thickness of Seam.		Specific Gravity.	Fixed Carbon.	Hygrom. Moisture.	Volatile Matter.	Ash.	Chemist.
	Miles.	*Feet.*	*Inches.*						
ILLINOIS.									
DU QUOIN, ...	254	6	10		61.20	7.00	28.60	3.20	Blaney.
MURPHYSBORO' . . .	250	3		1.353	57.30		38.29	4.50	Silliman, Jr.
DANVILLE, ... (Upper,)	170	6	06		53.10		43.20	3.40	Blaney.
" (Middle,)	"				51.80		41.40	2.80	"
" (Lower,)	"	6			55.60		33.20	11.30	"
ANVIL ROCK, (Average,)	60	4		1.273	57.90	7.60	29.50	3.50	Owen.
" (Upper,)	"	5	81	1.478	54.45	2.90	32.55	11.00	"
" (Middle,)	"	3	64	1.295	51.40	3.00	33.60	9.00	"
" (Main,)				1.309	50.50	2.00	36.00	2.50	"
" (Little,)					60.40		33.00	4.00	"
MORRIS, ...		4			57.20	11.00	23.80	8.00	Blaney.
"		5			67.40	10.40	23.00	9.20	"
LITTLE ROCK, (Upper,)	100	4	66		51.40	8.60	22.00	9.20	"
LA SALLE, (Middle,)	93	5			60.00	12.00	22.50	4.18	"
" (Lower,)		3			51.00	12.00	25.00	8.00	"
"					45.60	10.40	29.00	5.00	"
OHIO.	*From CLEVELAND.*								
HAMMONDSVILLE,	100	4		1.335	51.08		46.44	11.40	Newberry.
"	"				65.60		21.22	2.47	Blaney.
McINTOSH, ...	100	2	65	1.269	41.87		38.73	5.20	Newberry.
BRIER HILL, ...	80	4	66	1.309	61.24		33.56	16.39	"
TALLMADGE, ...	40	4	66	1.254	61.05		41.29	2.79	Mather,
CHIPPEWA, ...	50			1.251	61.05		41.29	2.23	Newberry.
BOLIVAR, ...	75			1.253	50.22		47.04	3.06	"
PENNSYLVANIA.									
PITTSBURG, ...	101	6		1.252	44.93		35.76	2.73	Johnson,
ORMSBY, ...					61.40		31.20	7.07	Blaney,
DARLINGTON, . . .	102	10		1.468	17.27		34.72	48.00	Newberry.

Limestones.—There is no dearth of these materials, whether required for construction or for burning into quicklime. The elevated ridges in the vicinity of Galena are capped by the Niagara limestone of a buff color, which is quarried in layers of various thicknesses, is easily wrought, and makes a handsome and durable building material. At the base of the bluffs on the Mississippi river, in the vicinity of Dubuque, a blue limestone of the age of the Trenton series, is quarried which affords a material equally desirable. These limestones though magnesian in their character, readily burn into lime.

At La Salle, the Coal Measures are capped by numerous layers of thick-bedded limestone which is extensively quarried.

At Kankakee, there are quarries in the Niagara limestone.

A few miles East of La Salle, in the Lower Silurian series, there is a band of hydraulic limestone, from which cement is largely manufactured.

The Chicago limestone, belonging to the Niagara group, forms the most beautiful material for construction in the United States. It possesses a warm yellow tint, and has not therefore the coldness of marble. It quarries in layers thin enough for flags, and thick enough for the most solid structures. It is free from grit, and may therefore be sawed, or chiseled into ornamental forms. Adjacent to water communication, the cost of transportation is slight; so that for building purposes, it affords a material combining alike cheapness, beauty, and durability.

From a point six miles above Jonesboro', and thence to Ullin, the underlying rocks are limestone, extending from the Carboniferous down to the Lower Silurian series. The Oölitic limestone near Jonesboro' affords a beautiful building material, but the lines of bedding are not distinct, which interferes with the successful quarrying. Most of these limestones readily calcine into quicklime.

Firestones.—The fine-grained sandstone near Cobden, in

the Sub-carboniferous series, yields excellent hearth-stones for furnaces.

Freestones.—At the base of the Coal Measures, near Makanda, the sandstone is of a uniform texture, and variously colored, buff, yellow and red. It is very durable, cuts readily, and has all the beauty of the Portland stone.

Iron Ores.—About two and one half miles west of the Illinois Central Railroad, and nearly four miles north of Jonesboro', on Section 34, Town 11 S. Range, 2 West of 3d P. M., being Railroad land, there occurs a ridge bearing east of north and west of south, which rises quite abruptly to the height of more than 200 feet above the valley. This ridge has appropriately received the name of The Iron Mountain. The base of the hill for 50 feet or more consists of fissile shale, succeeded by 80 feet of chert, intermingled with masses of hematatic iron ore, often in a state of great purity; the whole being capped by a cherty limestone 70 feet thick.

These deposits have been slightly explored, but there is little doubt that here is stored an inexhaustible supply of very rich ores, and under circumstances which admit of their being profitably wrought. These deposits belong to the Sub-carboniferous series.

Lead Ores.—Galena has long been known as the seat of the richest lead-bearing region in the United States. The Galena limestone, or lead-bearing rock, occupies a considerable area in Northern Illinois and Iowa, and Southern Wisconsin. Its position is between the Hudson river group and the Trenton limestone, and the lead deposits are restricted within that range. The present product of the mines is from 12,000 to 15,000 tons per annum, valued at from $1,500,000 to $2,000,000.

Brick.—In the timber regions, the sub-soil consists of such an admixture of clay and sand that it may readily be burned into brick. It is rarely that the clay requires any tempering of sand.

COST OF BUILDING.

Great misconception exists with regard to the difficulty of procuring building materials. Those who are unaccustomed to a prairie region suppose that the settler must be subjected to great inconvenience unless he has at least a forty-acre tract of woodland connected with his farm. Let it be borne in mind that the prairies are dotted with groves, and the streams are fringed with trees; and there are few points where fire-wood commands $4 00 per cord. Chicago is the greatest and cheapest lumber mart in the United States. A house of the style and dimensions of the one represented above—16 by 24 feet, $1\frac{1}{2}$ stories high, and containing five rooms—can be furnished complete and delivered on the cars for $200; put up within 100 miles of Chicago, plastered, painted once, and ready for occupancy, for $350. A good board fence of pine lumber, within 100 miles of Chicago, costs about 70 cents per rod. The price of fencing at this time at Chicago is from $9 00 to $9 50 per M. Shingles, best, $2 50 and $2 75. Lath, $1 50 to $2 00. Posts, per 100, $5 00 a $7 00. Good white-oak rails in the lumber region are worth from $2 00 to $3 00 per hundred; and it requires about 28,880 to fence a section.

FARMING IMPLEMENTS.

There is no region in the world which can be cultivated more economically than the prairies of Illinois. There are no stumps or stones to obstruct the plough or mower; and when once the prairie-sod is subdued, there remains a light pulverulent soil, which can be ploughed with a single horse. The long, gentle swells of the surface can be passed over without detriment by the various labor-saving machines. Already have these machines successfully supplanted the labor of human muscles, in planting, mowing, reaping, and threshing. The grand *desideratum* is THE STEAM-PLOUGH; and we do not despair of its accomplishment. Some of the best mechanical minds of the country are at work to solve the problem. At the next State Fair at least four steam-ploughs will be on exhibition. The Board of Agriculture of Illinois have offered a premium of $6,000 to the inventor of a successful Steam-plough, and the Illinois Central Railroad Company have super-added to it $1,500.

Reaping Machines are almost altogether used at the West. They cost $100 to $150. They will cut fourteen acres of wheat per day. Contracts for reaping are made at 62½ cents per acre. The contractor furnishes a driver, raker and horses; the farmer finds binders and shockers.

Threshing Machines will thresh three hundred bushels per day. It is generally contracted to be done at four to five cents per bushel, the contractor furnishing four horses and three hands ; the farmer, four more horses and five more hands, making in all eight hands, viz., one driver, one feeder, one measurer, one to pitch sheaves, one to cut bands, and three to take away straw.

The first class farmers' are substituting portable steam-engines for sawing, threshing, and other purposes.

Most of the agricultural implements are made in the State, and all that are desired can be procured at the agricultural warehouses in the principal towns. There is no necessity of importing them from the East. Besides, the prairie-ploughs require certain peculiarities of construction which distinguish them from all others. A good breaking-plough costs $16 ; common ploughs from $8 to $10 each. Ploughs made of cast iron will not work well in our soils, as it is impossible to keep them bright ; but those made of the best steel preserve their polish and work freely.

Ditching Machines.—With a view of benefitting the settlers on the Illinois Central Railroad lands, the Company have offered a prize of $500 for the best Ditching Machine; the State Board of Agriculture to be the arbiters. In the gentle depressions of the prairie, the surface-waters accumulate, and form what are provincially known as *slues*. By freeing the soil from this superfluous water, these lands may be converted into the finest meadows, and the health of the country greatly improved. The uplands may be rendered sufficiently dry by intersecting the surface with frequent furrows, and throwing up short slopes between them, without a resort to under-drains. So finely divided is the soil, and so free from roots and stones, that no serious obstacle exists to the introduction of some mechanical contrivance for draining the "slues," more expeditious and more economical, than the present method of spading; particularly, if it be applied during the wet season, when the ground is thoroughly saturated with water.

BREAKING AND CULTIVATING.

Notwithstanding the fertility of the soil, it is idle to suppose that the land is going to bring forth its increase spontaneously. God has not yet removed the doom placed upon our great ancestor : " In the sweat of thy brow, thou shalt eat bread." These lands are not cultivated, ordinarily, in a husbandman-like manner. The farmers plough only four or five inches deep, and consequently if the season is dry, the ·moisture cannot come up from ·beneath; and if the season is wet, the water has no chance to leach away. A hoe is seldom introduced into the corn-field, but a cultivator is once or twice during the season run between the rows, and followed by the shovel-plough.

The usual process pursued in subduing a farm is this : In the months of May and June the sod is turned over. It should be delayed until the grass has started, and finished before it has matured, as the roots sooner part with their vitality. In six weeks the sod will have rotted. It is then ready to be harrowed or cross-plowed, and sown with wheat. If the wheat is properly drilled, or harrowed in, it is ordinarily a good crop. To this should succeed corn for two or three years, and be followed by oats. Where .prairie is broken by the middle of May, it may be planted in sod-corn, and a yield of 15, 20, or 40, bushels per acre may be anticipated; but if the farmer has other corn-land, it is not desirable to resort to this crop. Many farmers use a breaking plough, which turns a furrow from eighteen to twenty-six inches wide, and about three inches deep, requiring a force of from three to six yoke of oxen. The plough is connected with a pair of wheels, and is self-regulating, so that it requires only a driver to manage it. The cost of breaking prairie is about $2 50 to $3 00 per acre. There is, however, no necessity of resorting to such a cumbersome force. A man with a pair of horses and a good plough, cutting twelve inches, can break an acre and one-half per day. And this may be done in the interval between planting and harvesting.

HEALTH.

The climate of Illinois is salubrious. Upon the prairies there is always a refreshing breeze; and those stifling, enervating heats, characteristic of the valleys and wooded regions, are comparatively unknown. The prevailing diseases are bilious; but they are of a mild type, and are easily managed. Fever and ague is apt to prevail where a soil, rich in organic matter, is for the first time turned up to the sun; but cultivation soon destroys the noxious gases which emanate from decaying herbage. The low bottom-lands and the dense groves which skirt the streams are apt to harbor miasma, and their shelter is to be avoided.

It must be borne in mind too, that, in subduing a farm, the settler deprives himself of comforts, and undergoes exposures at variance with his previous life; and if he finds himself in bad health, he is fain to attribute to the climate what in reality is the result of his own recklessness and folly.

Formerly the emigrant came to the state in a canvas-covered wagon which afforded him inadequate shelter

from the dews of evening, and the vicissitudes of temperature. He camped in the groves, and beside the sluggish
streams, that he might readily obtain wood and water,
where miasmatic vapors were sure to be generated. His
fare consisted of indigestible bacon and clammy bread.
He resorted for water to the surface pool, or the stagnant
stream. Arrived at his place of destination, he erected
a wretched cabin, through the chinks of which the winds
of heaven had free course. After all of these exposures, if
he had a "shake," he attributed it to the climate, rather
than to his own indiscretion. If at his former home he
had thus exposed himself, the same results would have
been sure to follow. Now, let the emigrant avoid the
groves where the pioneers settled for the purpose of ob-
taining timber; let him dig wells instead of resorting to
surface water; let him exercise a due regimen over his
diet, using the esculent vegetables with his animal food;
let him shun the strong draughts of night air after the
toils of the day; let him erect a comfortable frame house
instead of the common log-cabin; let him surround himself with cultivated fields, and pleasant gardens, and orchards of fruit,—and our word for it, he shall find that he
will enjoy a reasonable degree of health,—and that God
has not spread out these broad, fertile prairies to remain
uninhabitable by his creatures.

But instead of resorting to theory, we confidently ap-
peal to facts. The bills of mortality show that the average
duration of life is higher in Illinois, than in most of the
older states, or in most of the countries of the Old World.
She is in advance of Massachusetts, Connecticut, or New
York, which are regarded as healthy; and if we extend
the comparison to England, we find that, while in Illinois
less than fourteen in one thousand die, the average in
England is upwards of twenty-four in one thousand.

It may be said that, in Illinois the population is largely
made up of young and vigorous people from the older
states; but on the other hand let it be borne in mind, that

they are compelled to undergo hardships and exposures which they would not have encountered at home.

WATER.

In the hilly portions of the State, copious springs gush out from the surface. In the prairie region, this is not the case. Water, however, is ordinarily reached at a depth of from twenty to forty feet. Artesian wells have been successfully tried in some parts of the State. In Iroquois county, which consists of high-rolling prairie, not less than one hundred and fifty-four wells of this character have been bored; and instances are known, where, when the seam was struck, the force of the current was sufficient to bring up pebbles five inches in diameter. On the farm of Mr. Prentiss, near Onarga, the water is discharged through an orifice five inches in diameter, in a copious stream. This water is chalybeate in character.

These wells vary from 100 to 150 feet in depth, and pass through a blue clay into coarse gravel or quicksand beneath, which serves as a reservoir.

CROPS.

Indian Corn.—The surest, and perhaps in the long run the most valuable, crop raised in Illinois is Indian corn. The crop of 1857, was not less than 70,000,000 of bushels; and this year it will probably exceed 100,000,000. The cost of raising it is about ten cents per bushel, and the average yield is 40 bushels per acre. In favorable seasons some fields, when properly cultivated, yield 80 and even 100 bushels. One man and a boy can cultivate 40 acres, but two men with a boy can cultivate 100 acres. The farmers seldom carry a hoe into the field, but the weeds are kept down by the plough. When ripe, the corn may be harvested at any time; but it is usually done in mid-winter, as it receives no injury from standing in the hill. It is regarded in America as the staff of life not only for man, but beast. While it is dealt out liberally to the horse, the ox, and the pig, it forms an article of diet alike for the rich man and the poor. It is more nutritious and adapts itself better to the human system than wheat.

Our British relations have not yet learned that it is fit for human food, or even for horses; but that it may be safely used in fattening swine. The demand for this kind of grain, at once so cheap and nutritious, must largely increase with the increase of the human race, and of those animals so essential to our support.

Broom Corn.—This article flourishes luxuriantly on the black prairie-soil, and in the bottom lands of the Mississippi. There are specimens in the Land Department grown in the latter region, 18 feet in hight.

Wheat.—In that portion of the State south of the Terre Haute and Alton road, winter wheat is ordinarily a successful crop. The peculiarities of the wheat soil have been pointed out, in a previous part of this Pamphlet. The average yield is probably not less than 20 bushels per acre; but if the season be favorable, and the crop be put in with care, the yield may exceed 40 bushels. The harvest ordinarily commences about the 10th of June.

In the belt of country north of this line, and as high up as the Peoria and Oquawka road, the crop is less certain; and this uncertainty is due perhaps less to climate than to the mode of culture. The top soil, being composed of decayed vegetation and ashes deposited from the annual burnings, is light, with little adhesion between the particles. In dry weather, with a high wind, it drifts. By deep ploughing, bringing up the loam from beneath, a firmer and more compact soil is obtained, which will hold the rootlets of the plant more securely. The shoal ploughings of three or four inches simply stir up the loose ashes on the surface, and the winds blow away the particles of pulverulent earth from the roots of the wheat. Without asserting, therefore, that the central portion of the State is not adapted to winter wheat, we do say that the method of culture thus far pursued has not been successful. Winter wheat should be sown, or drilled in, late in August or early in September, that the roots may be thoroughly imbedded, and a mass of vegetation may spring up to serve as a winter covering against the action of frost.

The northern and central portions of the State are well fitted for the growth of spring wheat which is usually sown upon the broken sod of the preceding year, or on corn-stubble. It should be sown as soon as the frost is out of the ground, so that the straw may be stunted by the cold weather. The soil is so rich in nitrogenized organic matter that the crop is apt to run to stalk, the vesicles burst, and the ear does not fill; and hence ensue blight, chess, smut, and rust. The analyses furnished Mr. Caird show a deficiency of lime, and he suggests that its application would consolidate the soil, and impart strength to the wheat-stocks. The average yield of spring wheat is from 15 to 20 bushels per acre.

Oats is the product of a temperate climate, and hence they thrive best in the northern and central parts of the State, where the average yield is forty bushels to the acre, and often goes as high as eighty. They thrive best on ground that has been cultivated a few years, and should be harrowed in on land which has been turned over the preceding fall. The great danger is from a rank growth, producing a superabundance of straw, and hence early sowing is the best.

Barley thrives well, and is more or less saleable. If not required for brewing malt liquors, it may be profitably fed, the yield being about the same as oats. Many of the nations of Europe, particularly the Welsh, are fond of their home-brewed ale, and this is far better than corn-juice whiskey.

Root Crops, such as the turnip, the carrot, and the ruta-baga, may be easily grown in the rich, mellow soil of the prairie; but thus far their cultivation has been neglected, since corn is the most economical food that can be raised.

Hay Crop.—With so large a range of natural pasturage

about them, our farmers do not properly appreciate the value of the hay crop, when properly cured. It requires the exercise of as much care and judgment in gathering as any other crop. One farmer, by feeding hay, properly cured, may keep his stock in good condition through the winter; while another, dealing out hay which has been so thoroughly drenched by rain as to abstract all its juices, is compelled to feed with corn to keep his stock from becoming lean. With proper care, hay may be made the most economical food for stock during the winter. For this purpose, it should be cut while in flower, since in this state it contains the largest amount of sugar and gluten, which is the true source of nutriment. In curing hay, the object should be simply to dry out the water. The spreading of swaths is the first process; the cocking, after it shall be thoroughly wilted, is the second. The sweating process which it undergoes does not injure it, unless carried so far as to decompose the juices, causing them to pass off in the form of alcohol and carbonic acid gas, and rendering the hay itself " sour." As soon as cured, it should be stored, for nothing injures hay so much as drenching rains, since the juices are readily soluble in water. The successful introduction of mowing machines and raking machines has relieved the farmer of a vast amount of manual labor, and now the cost of gathering a ton of hay in Illinois need not exceed one dollar.

Timothy (*Phleum pratense*).—This is a very nutritious grass, and well fitted for exportation. The level prairie about Sandoval and Odin might be appropriated to its culture, from which points, after having been pressed, it might readily be sent to the markets on the Lower Mississippi. Being perennial, and deriving new vitality from the tubers each year, it yields a large return in proportion to the labor expended. It is not so well adapted to pasturage as some of the other grasses, as the sharp feet of cattle are apt to destroy the bulbs. The yield is between two and three tons per acre.

3

Hungarian Grass.—This cereal, first introduced by the Hungarian exiles, is becoming a favorite with the farmers, and the seed, from its scarcity, commands a high price. It requires to be put in with all the care of wheat. It matures in forty days sufficiently to cut, and becomes ripe in sixty days from sowing. It will answer to sow, therefore, in July, after the wheat crop has been removed. Two crops may be grown in the course of a single season. This is an excellent fodder, being as nutritious for horses as oats ; and cattle eat the stocks greedily after the seed has been threshed out. The yield is large, and, on the whole, it is as profitable a crop as the farmer can raise. Besides, the putting in of this crop occupies an interval of the farmer's time between the wheat-harvest and the corn-harvest.

Blue Grass (Poa pratensis).—This grass is preferred to all others by the Kentucky graziers. It is indigenous to the limestone soils of the West, and readily flourishes when transferred to the prairies of Illinois. It is not extirpated by the trampings of cattle. The usual method of pasturing is to turn cattle upon it in the spring and fall, but to take them off in mid-summer. This grass has this valuable peculiarity : it furnishes a light amount of stem, .but a large amount of leaves, which continue growing after the flowering stage, and hence afford almost perennial pasturage. In the middle portion of the State this grass yields food for eight months in the season, but as far south as Centralia it remains green during most of the winter.

It is the best method to lay down the ground in grass after it has been cropped for corn for three or four seasons, as the particles of soil acquire greater adhesion, and thus afford the roots a firmer hold.

Prairie Grass.—There are several varieties of prairie grass, but the most esteemed are the *Blue-joint,* which grows on the borders of the sloughs, and the *Red-top,* which seeks the high grounds. It starts early in May, and continues green until August. Early in autumn the tops become dry and wiry, but towards the roots the blades retain their greenness. It may be cut for hay in September and October, and stacked for winter use. The cost need not exceed one dollar per ton, where a mower is employed. In the spring and summer it affords excellent pasturage, and cattle thrive upon it. For fodder, it is not so good as the cultivated grasses which supplant it. It also ceases to be productive when it is closely pastured, or mowed for a few years in succession.

Potatoes.—The common potato, in the central and southern parts of the State, is not cultivated to a sufficient extent to form an article of export. Indeed, it seems to be out of its natural habitat. The finest potatoes we have ever seen were grown above latitude 48°, where the summer is only about three months in length. The St. Louis market is largely supplied from the colder clime of Michigan. In the northern part of Illinois it is an article of export.

Sweet Potato.—This plant matures as high up as Chicago, but in the latitude of Jonesboro' it grows to an immense size, and its peculiar flavor is developed in perfection.

STOCK-BREEDING, AND RAISING.

The prairies are well fitted for stock-raising in two essential particulars; the cheapness with which Indian corn can be grown, and the almost unlimited amount of natural pasturage. Jacob Strahn, who came to this country twenty-five years ago, a poor man, when in the full tide of enterprise, has been known to turn off 10,000 head of cattle a year. There are other graziers who range from 1,000 up to 5,000. One individual sends cattle to the eastern market to the value of $500,000 per annum. Many of the Kentucky and Ohio farmers are securing stock-farms on the Company's lands. One gentleman from the latter State has a tract of 22,000 acres which he is rapidly converting into a stock-farm, and another tract still larger, which he proposes to treat in the same way.

In the vicinity of Bloomington there are two stock-growers, brothers, who came to this State more than thirty years ago. They had nothing to rely upon but their strong hands and their far-seeing sagacity. One of them now owns 7,000 acres of land, 2,700 of which is in a high state of cultivation; and the yearly products of his farm, in cattle and hogs, often reached $50,000.

The other brother has 27,000 acres of land, 4,000 of which are in cultivation; and his annual sales of pork and beef reach $65,000.

These are examples of what industry and sagacity can accomplish upon these lands.

Considerable attention has been paid to cattle-breeding. Much good stock has been introduced from Kentucky and Ohio, and many fine bulls have been imported direct from England. The short horns are preferred for fattening; and of the bullocks turned off for market each year, the majority have never submitted their necks to the yoke.

The method of feeding is this. The cattle range over the prairie in the summer and fall. As the time approaches to fit them for market, they are fed in the open field from the standing shocks of corn. Prairie-grass, which has been mown and stacked the previous fall, is thrown out to them twice during each day. Two hogs are assigned to each ox to consume the undigested portions of corn.

It is the impression among the packers and graziers that the production of beef does not keep pace with the consumption, and that there is little fear of over-stocking the market.

There are English packers in the State who put up beef for the London market, where it bears a high character.

Swine.—Equal facilities exist for fattening hogs, and Chicago will, ere long, press close upon Cincinnati in this respect. It must be confessed, however, that our farmers manifest too great indifference with respect to the breed. Instead of the rounded proportions of the Sussex and Berkshire, we find that the stock have many of the qualities of the race horse.

Sheep.—It is only within a short period that our farmers have turned their attention to wool-growing—a branch of industry which is quite as remunerative as any in which he can engage. The flocks may range over the prairie for eight months in the year, in charge of a shepherd, but on the approach of winter they require the shelter of sheds, and to be fed from racks. The prairie-grass appears to be better adapted to sheep than any of the cultivated grasses. That pest of the flocks, the prairie-wolf, has now nearly disappeared. Ewes of the ordinary breed cost about $1 50, weathers $2 00.

The sheep, like man, adapts himself to almost every latitude; and hence he thrives equally well in every part of the State.

INDUCEMENTS TO SETTLE IN ILLINOIS.

Illinois holds out strong inducements to every young man of good health and correct habits, to settle within her borders. Before emigrating, he might as well make up his mind that he must for a time forego some of the comforts and conveniences to which he has been accustomed. If he has no capital, let him not hang about the towns, but go to work in the country where there is a demand for his labor, at remunerative prices. Let him buy no land, until he shall have accumulated enough money to pay for a team, to pay for fencing his farm, and erecting a comfortable dwelling. The great fault with our farmers has been, that they have bought more land than they could cultivate; and hence have become *land poor*.

Three years of labor will generally place him in funds to commence his career as a proprietor of the soil.

To the young farmer just starting in life, and with a capital of a thousand dollars, there is no better field for him to enter upon. At home, he has to encounter active competition, and work for unremunerative wages. If he cultivate the paternal acres, after years of toil, and after having reared and educated a family of children, he finds himself at the close of life, about where he started. Very many of the farms in New England do not yield five per cent. on the capital invested. They are so small as to make it undesirable to subdivide them among the children of the owner; and hence the farmer, in his declining years, so apportions his estate that one retains the homestead, while the others go out into the world to seek their fortunes. Let such an one, with his good common-school education, and his habits of thrift, come to the broad prairies and select a quarter-section, or 160 acres, at say $10 per acre, on the Company's terms of seven years' payment. For four years he pays interest in advance, the first installment being $96. He buys a yoke of oxen and a plough, which shall cost him $100. He erects a house to shelter him from the storm, for $350, and encloses forty acres with a two board-fence, to turn cattle, which shall cost him $150. If he join with a neighbor, he pays one-half. In May he turns over the sod of one-half of the tract enclosed, and puts in a crop of corn which shall yield .him fifteen bushels to the acre; but if he can rent some old land from a neighbor, it is better. In June, he breaks the other half, and early in September, he harrows in his wheat. With his remaining means, let him buy a few pigs and calves, or yearlings. The former he should pen up, but the latter may roam over the prairie. A few tons of hay mown from some neighboring meadow, together with his sod-corn, will carry his stock through the winter.

The second year, his twenty acres of corn-land will be mellow and ready to be re-planted. He encloses another forty acres, at a cost of $112 50, or if he remove the division fence, his expenses for additional materials will· be $75. He breaks an additional forty, going through the same routine. In July his wheat is harvested, which will yield him 400 bushels, worth from $300 to $400, and in October he finds himself in possession of 800 or 1000 bushels of corn, half a dozen fatted hogs, and others coming on to supply their places; his calves will have increased fifty per cent. in value, his steers will be ready to break, and one-half of his farm, or eighty acres, will be in a high state of cultivation, and his first broken land in a condition to put out in orchards, and everything will have assumed an air of comfort. The worst is now over. One-half of his farm is subdued, and will from henceforth, prove remunerative. The third year, he fences the whole 160 acres, by purchasing $75 worth of new materials, and removing the divisional fences. If he wishes to make a fence to turn hogs, he must add about thirty-three per cent. to the first cost. Again he breaks, and again goes through the same processes before described. He reaps his wheat, and gathers his corn. His calves have grown to cattle, his trees have taken root, his farm is now subdued and fenced, and he looks over his broad acres with a feeling of satisfaction, "I HAVE MADE MYSELF A HOME." The fourth year, he commences his payment of principal, and in the soil he finds himself possessed of ample resources to meet it.

Such is an outline of what a man of energy and a little capital can accomplish on these lands. The proprietor in his own right of a farm of 160 acres, properly fenced and cultivated, with a neat house, surrounded with gardens and orchards, and flocks and herds, he need not repine at his lot.

To the capitalist, these lands offer good opportunities for judicious investment. Their cultivation will afford a sure and profitable return, while their value will be rapidly enhanced from the great influx of population and wealth, and the consequent development of the agricultural and mineral resources of the State.

Lands in Ohio, Kentucky, and Indiana, equally eligible

to market, but less desirable in fertility, are held at from $60 to $100 per acre. The disparity is still greater if the comparison is extended to the Atlantic States. Now, in the progress of settlement, one of two things must take place; either these prairie-lands must rapidly rise in value to the standard in the older states, or the latter must fall until they accommodate themselves to the standard here. The true measure of value will be the productiveness of the land, *minus* the cost of transporting the products to market.

There is another class to whom these lands should prove attractive, to wit;—the middling farmers of England, Scotland and Wales. Deriving their origin from a common ancestry with us, speaking the same language, and linked to us by a common bond of sympathy, in religion, morals, and educational movements, these men would feel that they were casting their lot among friends instead of strangers. In setting forth the inducements to emigration, we prefer to use the language of one of their own countrymen, Mr. Caird, whose reputation as an accurate and competent observer cannot be questioned. We quote from his letter to Mr. Moffatt, Chairman of the London Committee of the Illinois Central Railway Company. He says :—

"To the young farmer who has to face keen competition at home, with rising rents and increasing wages, both a good thing to the country at large, but both likely to be accompanied by diminished profits to himself, the change will be this—that he may become the owner of better land in Illinois for the same sum as he would have to pay as a year's rent here ; that though manual labor is dearer, it is greatly economized by machinery ; and that the soil is so fresh and inexhausted that it requires no outlay for manures. Moreover, in the present state of that country, he need not purchase more land than he can crop, as he is free to graze his stock on the unoccupied prairie. It is this that constitutes one great advantage of settling on a prairie in comparison with a woodland country. In the latter, the settler can use no land until he conquer it from the forest ; in the former, he not only can at once put under crop all the land he purchases, but he is at liberty to pasture his stock and cut his hay without hindrance on all the unoccupied and fertile prairie which stretches around him. The grass and hay for his cattle thus cost him nothing, and though manual labor is dearer, horse-keep, which in England is such a heavy charge on the farmer, is very cheap. The skillful stock manager could not fail to make money, whether by cattle or sheep. Merino sheep are found very profitable. And, in regard to corn farming, if he considers that the average price of wheat in Illinois for the last ten years has been more than half that of England during the same period, whilst land of equal quality can be bought at less than one-thirtieth of the English price, he will see in a moment the immense disproportion between the value of the produce and that of the land in the two countries—and the chances which he thus has of an immediate profit, besides the farther great probability of such an early rise in the value of the land he buys as will tend to equalize the respective rates of profit in the two countries. The advantages which are offered to this class of purchasers by your credit system are very obvious. A young man cannot enter an arable farm of 300 acres in this country without a capital of nearly £2,000. Half that sum in Illinois will make him owner of the same extent of land, fenced, ploughed, and all under wheat. And if he avails himself of the Company's credit system, little more than £500 will be necessary to start him."

To the men of other nationalities, Illinois offers a cordial welcome and an hospitable home. The Dane, the Swede, the Norwegian, the Irish, the German, with his liberty-loving principles, in coming here, shall find those to whom he is connected by the ties of country, and with whom he can at once affiliate. To such men, *organized* emi-gration is preferable. Let them send a committee to the Land Department, and an examiner will be detailed to show them the Company's lands, and inform them where contiguous tracts can be secured. If the report is favorable, let the committee arrange for the arrival and settlement of the colony, by building houses, digging wells, and fencing farms, and providing all of those comforts and conveniences, which shall take away from the emigrant all unpleasant associations connected with his new home.

ROUTES TO ILLINOIS.

The principal ports in the United States at which the emigration is landed are New York, Boston, Portland, and New Orleans. The cost of passage across the Atlantic is from $100 and upwards, to $30 and below, dependent on the character of the accommodations. The map prefixed to this report will show the railway connections between Chicago, the seat of the Company's principal offices, and these points of departure. The following are the rates of fare at this time:—

FROM NEW YORK.

	1st Class.	2d Class.	Emigrant.
Via Hudson River, New York Central, Great Western (Canada), and Michigan Central, Railroads (distance 950 miles), affording the traveler an opportunity of visiting Niagara Falls and the Great Suspension Bridge over the Niagara River, without deviation from his route, ...	$23 00	$16 00	$10 00

If the traveler prefer, he may proceed

Via Hudson River, New York Central, Buffalo and Erie, Cleveland and Erie, Cleveland and Toledo, and Michigan Southern Railroads, (distance 963 miles).

Via New York and Erie, Buffalo and Erie, Cleveland and Erie, Cleveland and Toledo, and Michigan Southern Railroads, (distance 960 miles).

Via Camden and Amboy, Pennsylvania Central, and Pittsburg, Fort Wayne and Chicago Railroads, (distance 920 miles).

The fares in each case will be the same.

FROM BOSTON.

	1st Class.	2d Class.	Emigrant.
Via Boston and Worcester, Western, New York Central, Great Western (Canada), and Michigan Central Railroads, (distance 1010 miles), ...	$24 00	$14 00	$10 00

FROM NEW ORLEANS.

	1st	2d	Emigrant.
Via New Orleans, Jackson and Great Northern, Mississippi Central, Mobile and Ohio, and Illinois Central, (distance 962 miles),	$30 00	none.	none.
Via Steamboat to Cairo (1077 miles), thence by Illinois Central Railroad to Chicago (365 miles)—1442 miles, . . .	$30 00	——	$11 50

The cost of passage, during the past season, by "Train's Line," has been as follows:—

From Liverpool to Boston,	- - - -	$18.
From Gottenberg to Boston,	- - -	$20 to $24.

These are about the rates from these foreign ports to New York.

REMARKS

ON THE

SOIL AND PRODUCTIONS OF ILLINOIS.

[THE following remarks on the soil and productions of Illinois, have been prepared by M. L. Dunlap, Esq., of West Urbana, Champaign County, Illinois. Mr. Dunlap has been for twenty-three years a resident farmer in the State. For eighteen years he cultivated a nursery and farm at Leyden, Cook County, and for three years past has pursued the same course on a farm of two hundred and forty acres, three miles south of Urbana Station on the Chicago Branch of the Illinois Central Railroad. Having been connected for the past fifteen years with agricultural and other journals as editor or correspondent, he has become thoroughly familiar with the advantages, systems of agriculture, and results of cultivation, in all portions of the State, and is considered as an authority on these subjects. A practical farmer by profession, with long and varied experience, travelling repeatedly over all sections of the State as an intelligent and comprehensive observer, the accumulated results of his examination thus presented to the public, cannot fail to be of great advantage to all looking towards the selection of a western home.]

NORTHERN ILLINOIS.

Soil.—The leading feature of the soil in the northern part of the State is its resting on a stiff clay sub-soil nearly impervious to water. This sub-soil breaks up into small cakes when thrown up with the spade. When the soil is ploughed, say ten to thirteen inches deep, by trench-ploughing, that is, reversing the soil to that depth, and sub-soiled six or eight inches below this, then it is in a condition to absorb and carry off the surface water, and in case of drought to supply moisture from below by capillary attraction. On the other hand shallow ploughing, say from four to six inches, is ruinous to the farmer, as the crops are liable to injury by every change of weather. On this shallow ploughing, winter wheat is thrown out by frost; or the drying winds of March destroy the roots by robbing them of moisture. I apprehend it is not so much a want of lime in the soil, as a want of deep culture that shall provide for an equable distribution of moisture, that has made the growing of winter-wheat so unprofitable in this part of the State. Under-drains are too expensive to be used on wheat-lands; nor are they needed on our rolling plains, where deep tillage is effected, except as a means to carry off the surface water along the lines of depression. With this deep tillage and the necessary belts of timber to break off the March winds, winter-wheat can be cultivated profitably in this part of the State.

Spring Wheat and Oats.—These are favorite cereals, and have been found profitable even under a bad system of culture. The land for both requires nearly the same system of working: it should be powdered in all cases in autumn and wheat sown early in March; while the oats should be sown early in April, or in case of a late spring, immediately after the wheat. Thus the ploughing and sowing of these grains is done at a season of the year when the weather is favorable for team work and when other farm labor is not pressing.

Corn, and the System of Cultivation.— Let us take a piece of winter-wheat stubble that has been sub-soiled as indicated,—plough this in autumn, say three or four inches deep, just sufficient to bury the stubble and seeds of weeds. By spring this will have become rotted, and form a valuable manure; the previous sub-soiling will tend to make the surface dry and of course it can be easily ploughed in time to plant. This ploughing should be eight inches deep, and if well done, will bury the seeds of weeds below the point where they can germinate, and the after culture is quite easy.

As soon as the corn is ripe, it should be picked and husked, and now comes the question—What shall be done with the stalks? My answer is,—use them for drains. By placing a curved iron two inches wide, three-eights of an inch thick, and about twenty inches long, to the under side of the plough-beam and at right angles to it, fastened with a coulter clasp, the stalks will be brought within a small compass, and the furrow will even them completely. Thus, every fourth furrow will be laid with *corn-stalk-tile.*

Early in March, or so soon as the frost is partially out of the ground, this should be sown with spring-wheat and thoroughly harrowed in; if the ground is dry, rolling will be useful, but if wet otherwise. If the ground is muddy at the time of sowing, it is just as well, as the subsequent frost will make it mellow. The important point is to sow early, and have the soil well covered. This crop can be followed with oats; spring wheat should follow turnips and potatoes; sow oats on sod-land, or after wheat or barley, otherwise the straw is too rank and will lodge.

The Dairy.—But this part of the State, though it will produce the cereals at a good profit, is to be the great dairy district of the Northwest. Its natural adaptation to the grasses, the endurance and richness of its pasturage, the great stretches of natural meadow, the humidity of the climate, the springs of water, and the nearness to a large and growing city,—all point to this as the great leading feature of the productive farming industry of Northern Illinois, and to those who wish to make this their business, it offers the most superior inducements.

Fruit-growing.—Thus far, fruit-growing has not proved profitable in this part of the State. The severity of the winters has greatly damaged the orchards, unless well protected by belts of timber. At the same time, the garden fruits such as strawberries, currants, native raspberries, and the Houghton gooseberry, have done well; and no family need be without an abundance of these valuable fruits. The Clinton and Isabella grapes thrive well, where trained within bounds, and protected in winter.

Vegetables.—Irish potatoes, turnips, cabbages, and the usual garden vegetables thrive well in this part of the State. Sweet potatoes have of late been introduced and produce a fair crop, but are wanting in that richness that is acquired under the influence of a more southern sun. For domestic use, they will prove a valuable addition.

Sheep and Swine.—Sheep husbandry, unless with a view to mutton, must give place to the dairy; while pork raising must always form a part of the dairy products, and, though secondary, will yet go far to swell the profits of the farm, and add to the shipping values of the state.

Broom Corn, Flax, etc.—Broom corn has become a staple product, and enters largely among our articles of export, both in the brush, and manufactured into brooms. Flax is grown to considerable extent in the north-eastern part of the State, for the seed and also the lint, which in the form of tow is in demand in the city. Barley yields good crops, but the fluctuations in price have been such as to discourage its culture to some extent.

Manufactures.—The Fox, and Rock rivers form a continued series of water power, sufficient to build up hundreds of villages, which must make a ready home-market for a large part of our farm products, and give a denser population than will probably be realised by any other portion of the Northwest.

CENTRAL ILLINOIS.

Has a dryer climate, being out of the range of the lake winds, with a somewhat similar soil; but with a sub-soil of clay loam, in most cases permeable to moisture. These two points make a decided difference in the natural products of each.

Winter Wheat.—For winter wheat, this portion of the State has an advantage in the more perfect drainage of the sub-soil, making it less liable to heave out by winter frosts; but both parts of the State need the snow-covering which gives to the northern belt of winter grain its great protection; yet when sown here on a clover layer, timothy sod, or even prairie sod, it is comparatively a profitable crop.

Spring Wheat.—But we predict that spring-wheat will

be found equally, if not more profitable than winter-wheat, and that it must assume a prominent place in any system of rotation.

Oats.—In the strong loam, oats are apt to grow too vigorously, and are pretty sure to lodge; this has prevented their culture, and accounts for the almost total absence of this grain.

Corn.—There is no part of the world of the same extent, that is so natural to corn as this division of the State, and it may safely challenge all competition in this regard. The first field has yet to be pointed out that shows any sign of failure, however long it has been kept in corn, even without manure, and with the repeated ploughing under of the stalks it might be considered inexhaustible.

Grass and Pasturage.—Timothy and clover produce a large yield of hay, but are not so well adapted to pasturage. The blue grass luxuriates in this friable loam, and for eight months of the year produces the richest herbage. During the hot months, it is less luxuriant, but through most of the winter it will, if not fed close in the autumn, furnish a plentiful supply. Capt. J. N. Brown, who winters annually over seven hundred head of cattle and horses, says that he feeds less than half a ton of hay per head, and mostly when the weather is too inclement to allow the stock in the open pasture. This grass improves with feeding, and needs no breaking up and re-sodding for renewal. It is not adapted to meadows. With such a grass and corn-soil, it should be no matter of surprise that Central Illinois stands so high in the beef and pork-markets of the world.

Beef and the Dairy.—The dryness of the climate, the want of springs, the lack of succulent pasturage in the heat of summer, make this less desirable for dairying; while the cheapness of corn, the rich pasturage afforded by the blue grass for all except the hot months, give to stock-growing the advantage, and hence beef and pork are the great staples of this part of the State.

Vegetables require deep and thorough culture to with stand the heat of summer, and, with the exception of sweet potatoes, are not so sure a crop as in the north.

Fruits.—We now meet with a decided improvement in the productions of the orchard. Yet even here orchards will do better when protected by belts of timber, especially on the south and west. The peach-crop is not certain, yet often the trees are loaded to profusion. Grapes, with open thorough culture, and proper winter protection, will produce good crops. Raspberries, blackberries, and strawberries produce abundantly. The currant and gooseberry do not thrive so well unless shaded, the climate being too warm.

SOUTHERN ILLINOIS (Egypt).

As we proceed south on the Chicago branch of the Illinois Central Railroad, near Nioga, we observe a change of soil. Instead the blackish, or mulatto soil of Central Illinois, we now meet with the dull gray, or whitish soil of Egypt, the drift of which it is composed partaking largely of lime. Winter wheat takes the place of spring wheat; oats and barley flourish; corn is also a favorite crop. While Irish potatoes and vegetables make but a poor return, sweet potatoes grow luxuriantly. Apples and peaches produce abundantly; currants and gooseberries are more difficult of culture. Timothy produces a good crop of hay;—pasturage during the hot months is poor, water is more difficult to be had; and the products of the dairy are of an inferior quality. The mild winters are favorable to stock-growing. Hemp and tobacco grow well, but the great staple is winter-wheat, which is of superior quality. Cattle, hogs, and fruit thrive, of which peaches stand first and foremost in list of profitable products.

The Newton Pippin.—In that portion of Egypt north of the Big Muddy, the prairie-soil contains an excess of lime, and this is essential to the growth and perfection of this favorite American apple. Nowhere does this variety flourish better than in this lime-soil ; and in a few years, this section of the State will be more celebrated for this fruit, than the Hudson river valley or Pelham Farm, as here this variety attains a size and fairness unexcelled.

Apple Orchards.—From the adaptation of the soil, the mildness of the climate, and the ready access to markets, in every direction, these belts of lime-mud drift must ere long be mainly set to orchards ; as the demand for fruit, both north and south, must not only be constant, but increase in the direct ratio of the population. There is no part of the United States so natural to this fruit as this. Apples, pears, and peaches all grow bountifully ; but the apple will be the great staple, as a failure is never known, and partial failures seldom occur.

Timber.—South of the Big Muddy the land is densely timbered, and rolling, or broken into ridges. The soil is sandy loam, mixed with clay, and superior for the growth and the perfect maturity of the pear. Jonesboro', nearly in the centre of this tract, has a wide reputation for this valuable fruit. A large number of pear farms are opening, mostly in the high broken knolls ; but when this timber is cut away, so as to lower the frost line, nearly all the country will be found adapted to this fruit.

Generalities.—The subject of planting corn on prairie-sod, broken up in May and early in June, has been the source of much difference in opinion. Prairie in its natural state, when not previously pastured by stock, and broken up and planted at that season, will be found uncertain in its results, and is not to be recommended to the new settler ; but when this grass has been well fed down, it presents a very encouraging prospect of success. In this condition, it usually yields twenty to forty bushels of corn per acre, and will prove profitable. The soil before partially rotted, or destroyed by the tramping of cattle, will soon decay, and the ground will be in a good condition for the next crop. Whenever it can be done, it is desirable to pasture the prairie a year or two, before breaking. This has been my practice, and my best paying crops have been taken from prairie-sod on the first breaking.

It requires but a glance to convince us that the dairyman should locate in the northern part of the State; the stock grower in the central; the apple orchardist in the prairie portion of Egypt; and the peach grower and gardener in the southern, or timber portions :—not that any or all of these products cannot be grown in all parts of the State, but that in these particular locations, all of the elements of success are fully developed.

PROGRESS OF DEVELOPMENT.

It is impossible for a foreigner to realize the progress of development in the region north-west of the Ohio river. It is now a little more than seventy years since the first American colony was planted in that region. Since then, great and wonderful changes have taken place:—Seven states carved out of this territory and incorporated into the Union; cities founded, one of which exceeds 200,000, and one 120,000 in population, and several which exceed 50,000; villages planted at frequent intervals, with churches and school houses; wide tracts of forest leveled and converted into cultivated farms; roads and post routes everywhere opened; the bordering lakes and rivers floating a commercial marine equal to that of a second class power; the territory itself traversed by 8986 miles of railway, and constructed at a cost of $230,476,910; and an added population of about 9,000,000, or nearly one-third of the entire population of the United States. In the history of this period, there have been many commercial revulsions; but the region has always shown a recuperative power. Each census has exhibited a large increase in population, and a large development of material wealth.

INDUCEMENTS TO EMIGRATE.

[THE subjoined remarks are extracted from Caird's "Prairie Farming in America,"
—a work which at this time is exciting much attention in Great Britain. What he
says in reference to over-crowded population, and the enhanced value of land in the
Old World, is equally applicable to portions of the Atlantic States.]

"THE present position of the agricultural body in the United Kingdom is interesting and peculiar. The land-owner and the agricultural
laborer are both profiting by the same cause, a limited supply of the
commodity in which they deal. So long as this country continues to
prosper, the value of land must increase, for there can be no increase
of the land itself. But the demand for labor varies, and the supply is
subject to causes which render it uncertain. While, so long as the
present system of taxation continues, there must be a continued rise in
the value of land, there appears to me no equal certainty of a pro-
gressive advance in the rate of wages.

"But the hirer of land, the farmer, must inevitably suffer from the
continued competition for its possession. He has not only to meet his
own class, a necessarily increasing body, in this competition, but to
contend with men who, having made money in other pursuits, wish to
retire to the more pleasurable occupations of a country life. It is this
competition which is the true cause of the reduced profits of farming,
and this is more likely to increase than diminish. Great Britain is the
most attractive place of residence on the surface of the globe, whether
we regard its equable and healthy climate, its varied scenery and field
sports, the almost sacred character of the rights of property in the
eyes of its people, and the admirable combination of liberty and order
which is preserved under its political constitution. Men will pay for
these advantages, when they can afford it, a price which is not measur-
ed by the ordinary rates of profit.

"Besides this competition, which raises the rate of rent, the farmer
must now meet in his own market the produce of lower-priced foreign
lands. He will, no doubt, always have the cost of transport in his
favor, and this would generally be sufficient to balance the difference
of rent; but the land of this country cannot be cultivated without
manure, and the farmers of those foreign countries whose soil is rich
enough to yield corn for many years without manure, are thereby able
to undersell the British producer in his own market. The cost of
labor when the value of food of the working stock is calculated, is near-

ly the same at home and abroad, and superior fertility alone will be found to turn the advantage in favor of the foreign producer.

"The special adaptation of Britain for the production of live stock, and the constantly increasing demand for that branch of the farmer's produce, have hitherto modified the effects of foreign competition in corn: But even these, excellent though they have proved, cannot permanently counteract the cause of the farmer's diminished profits : viz., home competition for the possession of land. The soil here is now becoming more valuable for other purposes than ordinary farming, and the proportion between the producers and consumers of food is undergoing a rapid change. It appears from the Census that, in 1851, only 16 per cent. of the adult population of England was occupied in the business of agriculture. During the previous twenty years the proportion had fallen from 28 to 16 per cent., from no actual decrease of the numbers employed in agriculture, but from the far greater proportional increase of trade. The same gradual change is going on. At this time there is probably not more than one-tenth of the adult population of England employed in the culture of the land. The manufacturing, mining, and town populations are thus gradually absorbing the business of the country, increasing the value of the land, the profits of the landowner, but in the same proportion diminishing the area left for ordinary farming.

"The time seems thus to have arrived when the farmers must thin the ranks of home competition by sending off the young and enterprising to countries where they may become the owners of a fertile soil, and profitably contribute to supply the wants of the old country, whose land can no longer meet the demands of her dense population. During the last year we have imported into this country at the rate of nearly one million quarters of grain each month. We have thus in addition to our home crop, consumed each day the produce of TEN THOUSAND acres of foreign land, a demand so vast as to offer to young men of our own country the strongest inducements to take their share in its supply.

"Having, during last autumn, had an opportunity of making a pretty careful inspection of a part of the valley of the Upper Mississippi, probably the most fertile corn region in the world, I have collected for publication, in the form of a series of letters, the notes made by me at the time. There may be other countries which present equally good prospects to the agricultural emigrant. I venture to speak only of that which I have seen. This seems to me to offer the very field which we want at present,—a virgin soil of easy culture, with no forests to clear, of extraordinary natural fertility, in a country traversed by a most perfect system of railways, where no settler need be more than ten miles from a station, whose shore is washed by one of those great lakes through which an outlet is found to the Atlantic, and which possesses in the Mississippi itself a vast artery of commerce, navigable by steamers for thousands of miles. A great part of the country is underlaid with coal, iron, and lime, thus affording a present supply of such minerals, and the prospect of a great increase of value should the people ever turn their attention to manufactures. There is a complete organization of markets throughout the country ; and, setting aside the export to England, there is a very large and increasing local demand for every article of agricultural produce. The price of labor is economized by the most extensive and profitable use of agricultural machinery, and by the comparatively small cost of maintaining horses and working cattle. The grazing of cattle and sheep is very profitable, and the production of merino wool, already large, admits of vast increase.

"The fee simple of this land can be purchased at from 40s. to 50s. and 60s. [from $8 to $14] an acre.

" As a mere investment, this land would pay well to purchase and hold for a few years, and the increasing supply of gold, of which America herself yields an annual crop of ten millions sterling, will every year contribute to the higher relative value of land here and elsewhere. But the British emigrant, when he purchases this land, secures to himself not only the profits of farming it, but has also the growing increase in the value of the land itself, a right to which he can have no share at home. The country is now brought within a fortnight's journey from our shores, and is actually more accessible from Great Britain than most parts of Ireland were fifty years ago."

" There are two branches of his business to which I would specially ask the attention of the British emigrant to Illinois, viz. stock farming, and the cultivation of Indian corn. Full details will be found on both subjects in these letters. A good stock of cattle or sheep can be bought by a comparatively small outlay of capital; and, so long as the open prairie is thinly settled, grass for half the year may be had for nothing, and hay for the other half for only the cost of saving it. In regard to Indian corn, both climate and soil are more suitable to it than wheat. It can be grown to any extent, with a certain measure of success, every year, and, unlike wheat, this grain may be harvested with safety over a period of many weeks. A small and regular supply of labor thus suffices for the management of a large extent of land. There is always a market for it, and the lowest price at which we have ever seen it in England will afford a very good return to the prairie farmer of Illinois, after deducting all the charges of transporting.

"An emigrant from this country may be set down in Illinois at a total cost from Liverpool or Glasgow of 6*l.* 7*s.*, [about $30] inclusive of provisions.

"The present is a most favorable time for commencing to farm in Illinois. The panic of 1857 has not yet been forgotten, and the prices at which every sort of contract (building, fencing, ploughing,) may be executed, are 50 per cent. below the average rates."

THE LANDS AND HOMES OF THE WEST.
[*From the New York Tribune, April 21st,* 1858.]

As an almost unprecedented immigration is going forward to the rich and fertile prairies of the West, from the exhausted soils and overcrowded cities of the East, in consequence of the late commercial and business crisis, it is important to the farmer, the mechanic, and the laborer, who contemplates changing his home, to note the following facts:

1. No State in the Valley of the Mississippi offers so great inducements to the settler as the State of Illinois. Forming a part of that prolific belt which extends from the Atlantic to the Missouri river, and includes the States of Pennsylvania, Maryland, Ohio, Indiana, Iowa, and Northern Missouri, it holds a commanding and central position; while the great lake on one side, and the great rivers on the other, give it easy and equal access to the North, the South, the East and the West.

2. The climate, removed alike from the rigorous severity of the more northern States, and the oppressive heats of the more southern, is both salubrious and agreeable. According to the federal census of 1850, the rate of mortality in Illinois is less than in several of the New England States. The soil, composed of a deep, rich loam, is as fertile as any on the globe. It is, for the most part, so easily worked—requiring no grubbing up of stumps and picking off of stones—that the labor of one man is as effective, commonly, as that of two or three men on the rockier soils of the East, and far more productive. One man on the prairies can break from two to three acres, and afterward plough from six to eight acres per day, while in the East he can only break from one-half to one acre per day, and plough from two to three acres afterward. The yield of the prairies, at the same time, is nearly three-fold greater. In fact, Illinois was long ago designated by popular instinct as the Garden State of the West; 'and now that it

has been brought so extensively under cultivation, it more than ever deserves the name.

3. Illinois is not a frontier State, in which the settler is exposed to the severe privations and hardships of early settlement, but it contains over a million and a half of residents, numerous cities, towns, and villages, and 2775 miles of completed railway, which is more than any other State of the Union has, with the exception of New York and Ohio. Ninety millions of dollars have been expended on works of internal improvement, without resorting to a State debt, and to consequent taxation; and 1,800,000 acres of land have been devoted to purposes of education and general utility. These improvements will supply a revenue to the State for the public expenditures for all time to come, and consequently taxation will be merely nominal.

4. It is often said that Illinois is unwooded; but the fact is, that there is scarcely a county in the State without considerable forests, while the southern part of it alone contains 2,000,000 acres of timber. In the year 1857 there was brought into Chicago 460,000,000 feet of lumber. Chicago is also the greatest grain depository in the world, and is the terminus of 3953 miles of finished railway. In different parts of the State, iron, coal, and fine building stone are found in abundance.

5. Nowhere can excellent land be procured on more favorable terms than in Illinois. The Central Railroad Company, to which the State granted the 2,590,000 acres which had been donated by the General Government—extending through the centre of the State, north and south, fifteen miles on each side of the railroad—having disposed of 1,200,000 acres, offers the rest at moderate prices, on long credits and moderate rates of interest. The prices vary from $6 to $30, and the credits extend over a period of seven years.

6. There are on the line of the Central Railroad 100 cities and villages, with populations varying from 200 to 12,000 souls—with factories, mills, stores, post-offices, schools, and churches—all rapidly growing in numbers and wealth, and affording the comforts of civilized life to the settler, while they open every opportunity and prospect of business to the mechanic and trader. The counties contiguous to the road embrace a population of over 600,000, for the most part thrifty, enterprising, and industrious.

7. Thus it will be seen that the lands of Illinois are largely peopled and cultivated; their products are within easy reach of all the great western centres of trade, and may be transported, by way of the lake, to the Eastern markets, at less cost than from many intermediate points; and though these lands are now sold for from $6 to $30 per acre, they must inevitably advance to $50, and even $100, within a few years. Lands that were lately sold by the Company for $15 or $25 per acre will now bring from $50 to $100. The Illinois Central Company gives no encouragement to speculative purchasers, for its own interests prompt it to prefer the actual settler, who raises the value of neighboring lands, and contributes to the traffic of the road.

56

Statistics of Towns on the

Name of Town.	Organized.	Inhabitants, 1850.	Inhabitants, 1856.	Inhabitants, 1859.	Houses, 1856.	Houses, 1859.	Churches, 1859.	Schools, 1859.	Stores, 1859.	Hotels, 1859.	Saw Mills, 1859.	Four Mills, 1859.	Factories, 1859.	Acres In Wheat, 1855.	Acres In Wheat, 1858.	Acres In Wheat, 1859.	Acres In Corn, 1858.
Northern Division.																	
Dunleith,*†	1853	5	1.800	2 000	2,000	50	2	2	15	7	3		4	1,000	1,000	1,000	300
Menomiuee,	No	town	laid	out	yet.									200	500	500	100
Galena,† *	1835	6,000	12,000	15,000	2,500	3,100	13	25	213	21	3	2	41	13,000	15,300	17 400	1.000
Council Hill	1828	3.0	500	300	120	75	2	1	2	3		1		7,000	2,000	2 000	4,000
Scales Mound,*	1850	14	292	300	40	10	2	2	3	2		1		6,000	6.300	5.700	10.400
Apple River,*	1854	None	200	250	40	56	2	1	3	1				3 600	7.000	8.000	2 500
Warren,†*	1850	25	800	1,100	150	325	2	3	19	1		1		6 000	8,000	10,000	6.000
Nora,*	1852	None	400	600	78	104	4	4	3	2		1		10.500	20,0 0	30.000	5.200
Lena,*	1853	5	350	750	116	150	5	2	8	1	8	1		5 000	8.000	8.000	2.000
Eleroy,	1850	18	750	250	150	62	2	1	4	1				8.000	10 000	12.000	4 0 0
Freeport,†*	1838	1.40.	6,000	7,000	1,600	1,800	11	11	70	9	2	3	12	22 000	45.000	5 000	15 000
Crane's Grove,	No	town	laid	out	yet.									6,000	11,0 0	15.000	7 000
Forreston,*	1855	None	153	425	30	110	1	1	6	2			3	9,000	20.000	25.000	6.500
Haldane,	No	town	laid	ont	yet.									3.000	8.000	4 000	2.000
Polo,†*	1854	None	2.500	3,500	500	750	6		35	4	4	4		12.000	18,000	21.000	9.000
Woosung,	1855	None	105	123	30	33		1	3	1	1			1.450	2.000	3 270	3 800
Dixon,†*	1839	640	4.500	3.500	515	550	7	6	63	6	2	3	8	20.000	8,600	5.340	24.000
Amboy,*†	1850	16	2 500	3,000	350	380	4	3	20	3	1	2	3	22.000	9.000	10 500	34 000
Sublette,*	1855	None	1.098	1 300	158	300	2	9	2			1		3.800	12.000	25.000	3.060
Mendota,†*	1853	None	1,400	3.000	242	700	7	6	40	7		1	4	25,200	55.000	60.000	32 400
Homer,	No	town	laid	out	yet.									6.000	17.000	8.000	9.000
La Salle,†*	1839	200	7,250	8,100	1,550	1,960	10	15	150	7	2	3	15	7.000	11.000	9.000	20.000
'onica,	1850	3	240	800	60	150	3	4	8	2				21,500	23 500	24 500	23.500
Wenona,*	1855	None	1,200	600	300	100	2	1	6	2				2,400	6 000	70.000	20,300
Rutland,*	1856	None	70	170	12	26	1	1	1	1				4.360	11.600	12,000	8,000
Minouk,*	1854	None	130	180	28	35	1	1	4	1	1			6 700	40,000	50,000	5,100
Panola,*	1853	None	195	250	39	45	1	1	6	1			1	15,000	30,000	52 000	12,000
El Paso,†*	1857	None	600	None	120	1	2	5	3		2			6,000	15.000	13,000	2 000
Kappa,*	1853	None	2 8	165	47	48	1	3	1	1	1			12.740	7.500	8,480	30.100
Hudson,*	1836	25	110	212	23	42	2	1	5					10,000	16,950	15,540	20 000
Bloomington,†*	1832	2.200	7,000	8,500	2,986	3,200	16	21	125	12	1	3	40	4,000	70,000	70,000	45,000
Heyworth,*	1856	None	200	300	20	64	1	1	2	2		1	1	20,000	20,000	23,000	15,000
Wapella,*	1853	None	350	400	73	80	1	1	8	2		5		11.200	30 000	35,000	21,500
Clinton,†*	1845	800	1,000	2,200	350	500	3	6	20	3	4	2	2	2,500	23,000	12,000	32,000
Maroa,*	1855	None	28	130	3	21	1	1	3	1				8,500	8.000	4 000	4.000
Forsyth,	No	town	laid	ont	yet									1,200	3.000	4,200	3,000
Decatur,†*	1829	600	4,000	7,000	600	1,150	13	7	98	9	2	4	14	24,000	50,000	40,000	50,000
Macon,*	1854	None	28	30		3		1						3,000	4,000	2,000	500
Monwequa,*	1553	None	400	375	150	85	3	1	12	2	1	3		25,000	50,000	30,000	4,000
Assumption,*	1855	None	40	400	7	40	2	1	5	1		1	2	2,000	15,000	1,000	4,000
Pana,†*	1855	None	650	798	86	171	2	1	13	4		1	1	2,000	8.000	6,000	12,000
Oconee,*	1855	None	80	117	22	22	1	1	6	2		2	8	1,300	4,000	4,000	20,000
Ramsey,*	1856	None	75	150	10	30	1	1	3	3	2			6,200	12.000	10,000	15,6 0
Vandalia,†*	1820	300	1,000	1,800	265	300	4	1	18	4	1	2	1	1,000	12,000	14,000	4,000
Shobonier,*	1856	None	23	55	3	10	1	1	1	1	1	1		1,500	4,000	5,000	3,000
Patoka,*	1855	None	80	60	5	14	1	4	1					400	3,000	4,000	1,500
Sandoval,†*	1854	None	120	400	30	60	1	1	4	5				300	2,000	4,000	1,400
														442,390	810,750	846,030	567,060

* Stations supplied with Maps of vacant lands belonging to the Railroad Company, with prices. Parties wishing to examine lands belonging to the Company can apply to the Railroad Station Agents for information and assistance. *No other agencies are recognized by the Land Department.*
† Telegraph Stations.

The above tables are intended to set forth the condition of the railroad Towns, with the territories tributary to them, on or about July 1, 1859. At some of the stations, small settlements existed before the organization of a town, which accounts for population appearing on the statement, in a few instances, before the date given for its organization.

In making up the returns for 1856, a few of the agents sent in statistics of population and buildings embraced in a whole township, as if contained in the town limits only. These errors have been corrected in the returns for 1859, and therefore the tables show an apparent decrease in the prosperity of some places, such as Council-Hill, Wenona, Manteno, Chebanse, Jonesboro', &c.; whereas, the increase at these points has been really very considerable. The floating population of laborers, &c., is also reckoned in these returns, and this may be distributed at any time to other points. It does not, however, materially affect the general result.

Illinois Central Railroad.

Acres in Corn, 1858.	Acres in Corn, 1859.	New Farms opened, 1856.	New Farms opened, 1858.	New Farms opened, 1859.	Estimated Value Stock, 1855.	Estimated Value Stock, 1859.	Total Population 185 5.	Total Population 1859.	Places of Nativity of Majority of Settlers.
250	1,000	2	5	10	$3.000	$5.500	1,500	3,000	Germany and Ireland.
800	400	1	3	2	2.000	5.000	200	250	New England.
1.560	1.980	19	12	5	104,400	223,300	25,00	45,000	New York and New England.
2,000	3,000	50			25,000	30.000	400	650	England.
8.000	9,100	72	18	11	65.000	80.000	2,500	3,000	England and Germany.
2.500	3.000	70	10	4	20.000	80,000	140	270	British Islands.
8.000	9 000	50	75	25	10.500	20,000	450	2 500	Ohio and New York.
20,000	30.000	80	18	10	19.500	82.500	400	1.100	New York.
2.000	4,000	17	20	12	200,000	300 000	4,000	5,000	Vermont.
9.000	12.000	13	6	8	3 300	23,100	2.5	800	Ireland and Germany.
40,000	45.000	65	100	100	120.600	200.000	15,000	30,000	New England.
13,000	12.000	10	7	2	35,000	50,00	250	325	New York and Pennsylvania.
14,000	18 000	49	41	50	45,000	125.000	90	425	Pennsylvania.
7.000	8,000	17	4	2	25.000	30.000	40	110	New York and Massachusetts.
11,000	12.000	60	100	200	20.000	50,000	6,000	12,000	New York and Maryland.
3.000	5.200	34	17	4	4.000	20,000	54	425	New England.
7.500	10.650	80	10	25	191.800	186,100	4,707	7,602	Pennsylvania.
7.000	8 500	70	35	30	60,000	100,000	8,000	10.500	New England.
15.000	30,000	5	20	50	200 000	450.000	2.000	3 000	New York.
60,000	70 000	100	150	75	15 000	45,000	1 800	5,000	Ohio and Germany.
20,000	18,000	84	11	4	19,000	25,000	300	450	Ohio and Pennsylvania.
30.000	35.000	25	20	30	80.000	360.000	10,000	12,000	Ireland and Germany.
30.500	15.500	180	100	100	150,000	200.000	1,000	2.800	New England.
30.000	40.000	100	75	75	40.000	50.000	1,200	6,000	Middle States.
6,500	13,800	128	60	20	5.000	95,000	57	1,200	Vermont.
15.000	25,000	179	150	75	8.000	50,000	200	2.000	Middle States.
16,000	30,000	100	20	30	100,000	100.000	2,500	3,000	New York.
30.000	54.500	73	15	20	12,000	50,000	60	450	New York.
15,000	12.000	60	15	6	60,000	40,000	2,000	1,800	Ohio.
24,000	31,220	21	35	20	50,000	80,000	1,200	2,400	Ohio.
65,000	95.000	400	200	200	500,000	1,250,000	18,000	24,000	Ohio and Kentucky.
30,000	35.000	70	25	10	75.000	125,000	1,400	2.500	Ohio.
40,000	60.000	140	20	100	300.000	1,000,000	3,000	6,000	Ohio and Kentucky.
20,000	25.000	75	25	20	378,000	630.000	8,500	11,500	Ohio and Kentucky.
4,000	12,000	26	20	10	15,000	60,000	400	1,500	Illinois and Ohio.
7,000	18,000	19	5	2	10,000	35,000	60	480	Pennsylvania and Kentucky.
70,000	1,0,000	100	100	50	160.000	250,000	6,000	12,000	Pennsylvania and Ohio.
600	2,000	38	6	1	12.000	20,000	75	200	New York.
5,000	40,000	30	60	20	172,000	400,000	750	4.000	Kentucky.
18,000	20,000	25	30	40	60,000	180,000	59	4,000	Canada and Louisiana.
20,000	30.000	25	65	20	253,000	344,800	250	1,482	Eastern States.
20.000	25.000	15	3		65,000	200,000	1,000	1,500	Tennessee and Kentucky.
20,000	23.500	6	10	6	149,700	295,200	5	150	Tennessee and Kentucky.
10,000	12,000	20	25	10	20,000	60,000	5,000	9.000	Kentucky and Tennessee.
3,000	5,000	15	17	21	10,000	30.000	1,000	1,000	Ohio and New York.
4,000	8,000	7	6	14	15,000	18,000	800	500	Kentucky and Tennessee.
1,500	1,500	10	15	20	50,000	120,000	1,500	1,800	Ohio, Kentucky and Tennessee.
786,210	1,100,180				$3,937,600	$8,099,500			

The statistics of the Towns proper are embraced in the first thirteen columns; the remaining fourteen having reference to the territory fairly to be considered as tributary to each station.

The areas in cultivation have been estimated by parties at each station well acquainted with the surrounding country, and reference has been made to the assessors' books whenever this was practicable. The valuations of stock have generally been obtained from this source, and should be considered as varying from thirty-three to fifty per cent. below the true value. In some localities, owing to the establishment of new Stations, part of the territory included in the previous returns from one Station, has been transferred to another.

Corn and Wheat being the great staples of Illinois, the most prominent positions have been assigned to these products. In the Northern part of the State, Oats is an important product of agriculture, in some localities occupying an equal area in its cultivation with either Corn or Wheat. So, also, of Fruit, in the Southern part. About Makanda, for instance, over 10,000 acres are planted with peach trees; and in 1858, 156,000 bushels of peaches were shipped from Cobden station alone; while the shipments of this season will

Statistics of Towns on the

Name of Town	Organized	Inhabitants, 1850.	Inhabitants, 1856.	Inhabitants, 1859.	Houses, 1859.	Houses, 1859.	Churches, 1859.	Schools, 1859.	Stores, 1859.	Hotels, 1859.	Saw Mills, 1859.	Flour Mills, 1859.	Factories, 1859.	Acres in Wheat, 1855.	Acres in Wheat, 1858.	Acres in Wheat, 1859.	Acres in Corn, 1855.
Chicago Division.																	
Calumet,†	1833	50	247	50	56	5	1	1	3	3	1			200	200	100	600
Thornton,*	1853	None	168	260	31	53	1	1	3	3				700	1,040	1,200	1,100
Matteson,	1856	None		98		24	1	3	1					1,200	4,000	4,750	2,000
Richton,	1853	10	500	1,000	47	250	3	7	5	3				800	4,000	4,500	3,000
Money,†*	1850	145	800	840	80	87	1	6	6	2	1	1	1	700	2,240	2,400	4,500
Peotone,*	1856	None	34	24	8	9		1	1					3,500	2,600	3,000	3,400
Manteno,*	1854	None	750	500	200	74	1	1	8	2				10,600	11,000	11,000	14,500
Kankakee,†*	1853	None	3,640	4,000	820	940	9	9	50	6			7	6,000	31,000	43,000	10,000
Chebanse,*	1854	None	600	70	125	17		1	3	1				260	10,000	15,000	1,500
Clifton,*	1857	None	None	175	None	20	1	1	2	1	1			1,000	2,000	4,000	3,000
Ashkum,*	1855	None	50	444	6	45	2	2	4	2	1			5,250	12,000	6,000	1,800
Gilman,†*	1857	None	None	130	None	35	1	1	3	2				300	500	2,000	700
Onarga,*	1854	None	320	600	64	125	3	3	11	2		1	1	3,000	5,000	12,000	8,100
Spring Creek,	1852	15	110	140	45	20		1	1		1	1		1,000	2,500	3,000	2,340
Bulkley,*	1859			17		3			1					600	1,700	2,000	800
Lodu,*	1855	None	174	900	31	130		2	8	2		1	1	400	2,500	1,300	300
Paxton,†*	1857	None	15	400	3	65	1	1	6	2				2,000	4,000	15,000	16,000
Pera,*	1855	None	28	39	4	8		1	2					210	800	1,000	2,460
Rantoul,*	1856	None	125	90	21	18	1	3	1					4,240	4,000	5,700	2,000
Urbana,†*	1835	500	3,285	4,000	367	950	8	5	54	8	2	2	3	5,580	20,000	20,000	12,000
Tolono,†*	1856	None	None	550	None	110	3	1	5	3				2,600	10,000	12,000	5,000
Pesotum,*	1854	None	33	60	5	9		1	2					3,140	8,000	12,000	4,270
Tuscola,*	1857	None	None	105	None	30	1		6	1				2,830	6,400	10,500	3,700
Oraw,*	1855	None	20	350	4	70	2	2	6	2				1,500	50,000	50,000	60,000
Milton,*	1857	None	5	31	2	6		1	1					1,000	3,000	3,000	16,000
Muttoon,†*	1855	None	472	1,400	113	400	3	3	80	3	1	1	2	2,000	8,000	5,000	65,000
Neoga,*	1856	None	16	130	5	27	1	3	1		1		1	3,000	4,000	3,000	42,000
Effingham,†*	1855	None	200	300	41	60	1	3	8	3				5,000	10,000	18,000	12,000
Watson,*	1856	None	25	40	6	7		1	2	1	1	1		500	500	500	2,000
Mason,	1855	None		200		47	2	1	7	1	1		1	4,000	6,000	8,000	17,000
Edgewood,*	1856	None		48		8		2	2	2				1,700	5,000	6,500	11,000
Farina,*	1856	None		50		9		1	2	1				3,000	6,000	9,370	10,000
Kinmundy,†*	1855	None		300		73	1	1	7	1	1	1	2	800	1,000	6,500	5,000
Foonti,*	1856													1,800	12,000	10,000	9,400
Olin,†*	1856	None	5	40	1	4		1						740	1,800	2,000	14,000
Central City,	1853	None		650		200	3	2	5	1			1.15	2,000	8,000	4,000	12,000
Centralia,†*	1854	None	1,900	2,500	275	325	3	2	20	7	1	2	1	1,500	12,000	14,500	5,000
Richview,*	1840	65	718	1,200	156	250	2	3	9	2	1			3,000	20,000	20,000	35,600
Ashler,†*	1854	None	300	1,000	100	150	2	2	6	3	1	1	10	2,000	8,000	10,000	8,000
Coloma,*	1856	None	113	121	24	26	1	1	4	1				1,000	4,300	4,300	8,000
Tamaroa,*	1854	None	60	400	17	106	1	1	12	4		1		4,200	8,000	9,000	18,000
St John's,†	1857	None		548		71	1	2	1	1				2,400	3,240	3,080	3,240
Du Quoin,†*	1853	None	300	1,200	40	300	2	4	22	3	1	2		2,000	6,000	6,600	12,400
De Soto,*	1854	None	500	800	50	175	2	2	8	3	2	2	4	4,320	5,000	6,500	12,000
Carbondale,†*	1853	None	700	1,100	110	220	2	3	16	3	2	2	15	3,000	5,000	6,000	6,200
Makanda,*	1854	14	50	43	4	8		2	1	1				4,200	10,000	5,000	4,500
Cobden,*	1857	None	6	150	2	37	1		4	1				7,000	7,000	8,000	12,000
Jonesboro',†*	1818	584	1,209	700	263	120	1	1	9	2		1		21,000	16,000	23,000	43,000
Dongola,*	1857	None	None	150	None	24	1	1	5	1	7	2	3	9,000	12,000	15,000	10,000
Wetang,	1856	None	120	185	23	34	2	3	1	1	4	1		7,200	7,000	7,000	6,000
Ulin,*	1854	None	250	325	33	35	1	1	3	3	6		1	1,000	1,000	2,000	25,000
Pulaski,†*	1854	None	150	201	30	30	1	1	2	3		2		3,000	8,000	9,000	4,100
Villa Ridge,	1854	None	93	72	12	25	1	1	3	1	2			2,000	5,000	7,000	4,000
Mound City June'n																	
Cairo,†*	1853	300	3,000	5,200	400	590	4	4	00	20	3	2	10				
														160,840	393,320	473,250	695,510

! Town laid out, but no improvements yet made. ¶ A few houses only, occupied by Irish laborers, &c. No town laid out yet. ‖ No agricultural country tributary to it. | No agricultural country tributary to it.

probably considerably exceed that amount. Jonesboro' also ships large quantities of peaches, as well as vegetables and berries from the extensive market gardens located near the town. About 1,500 hogsheads of tobacco will be shipped this season from Makanda station.

Extensive Coal mines are worked at La Salle, St. John's and Du Quoin stations ; also at Bryant, on the Great Western Railroad, about thirty miles east of Tolono station.

Illinois Central Railroad.

Acres in Corn, 1858.	Acres in Corn, 1859.	New Farms opened, 1856.	New Farms opened, 1858.	New Farms opened 1859	Estimated Value Stock, 1856.	Estimated Value Stock, 1859	Total Population 1856.	Total Population 1859	Places of Nativity of Majority of Settlers.
1,000	1.000	10	10	15	$6,000	$10,000	150	250	Holland and Germany.
3,000	4.500	9	8	13	14,000	21,000	430	1,250	Germany.
5,000	5.500	32	6	5	20,000	35,000	600	700	Germany.
6,000	7,000	10	12	14	35,000	80,000	350	1,000	Germany.
7,000	7,800	11	9	6	20,000	80,000	350	840	Connecticut and Germany.
5,000	6,000	8	2	5	9,000	16,000	200	500	Pennsylvania.
20,000	25,000	50	50	25	60,000	120,000	3,000	5,500	Mass., N. York and Canada.
61,000	97,000	300	320	850	482,700	632,400	10,010	21,500	New England.
20,000	40,000	40	20	35	2,500	50,000	200	1,500	New York and Massachusetts.
4,000	10,500	16	75	45	4,000	6,000	800	3,000	Massachusetts and Canada.
10,000	19,000	58	106	122	11,000	32,000	500	1,300	New York.
1,800	10,050	17	3	5	2,000	25,000	30	500	Kentucky.
10,000	15,000	62	10	2	10,000	50,000	400	1,800	New England.
4,000	6,000	40	15	12	10,000	30,000	500	1,000	Ohio and Tennessee.
8,000	12,000	7	3	1	15,000	30,000	60	400	New York and Pennsylvania.
5,000	20,000	105	23	3	20,000	50,000	200	1,500	N.England and Middle States.
25,000	40,000	35	25	15	200,000	300,000	2,000	5,000	New York and Ohio.
2,000	2,500	26	1	1	20,000	25,000	21	39	Kentucky and Ohio.
5,000	13,500	84	50	20	100,000	111,000	100	630	Ohio.
15,000	50,000	117	125	100	340,500	625,400	4,000	8,000	Kentucky and New York.
20,000	30,000	41	43	35	17,800	250,000	300	17,500	Ohio.
15,000	20,000	78	15	18	125,000	500,000	300	1,500	N. Y., Penn. and Kentucky.
12,150	30,130	23	8	18	75,000	100,000	500	2,500	Kentucky and Indiana.
60,000	80,000	20	10	12	15,000	100,000	500	2,000	Ohio and Pennsylvania.
20,000	25,000	27	15	3	10,000	50,000	500	1,300	Virginia, Kentucky and Ohio.
30,000	60,000	18	51	40	102,000	150,000	2,500	7,500	Kentucky.
4,600	8,000	34	30	10	18,500	60,000	250	1,450	Indiana and Germany.
9,000	40,000	20	100	50	40,000	100,000	6,000	10,000	Ohio, Indiana and Germany.
5,000	21,000	16	20	17	10,000	10,000	700	700	New York and Pennsylvania.
25,000	30,000	35	20	40	60,000	100,000	25	200	Ohio and Indiana.
15,000	25,000	15	60	75	150,000	225,000	3,000	5,500	N.Y., Kentucky & Tennessee
16,000	22,400	14	17	40	20,000	100,000	480	2,200	Ind., Ky., N. Y. and England.
8,000	15,000	40	24	25	10,000	20,000	1,000	1,700	Ohio and Tennessee.
20,000	25,000	11	8	5	40,000	50,000	3,200	4,000	Tennessee.
300	600	37	6	8	1,000	3,000	50	400	Ohio.
15,000	25,000	29	25	38	250,000	300,000	2,500	3,000	Ky., Tennessee and Vermont.
6,650	8,000	90	25	50	1,040,000	1,680,000	20,000	30,000	New England.
50,000	50,000	50	100	100	200,000	350,000	3,000	5,000	Tenn., N. Y and N. England.
10,000	12,000	50	50	50	300,000	450,000	10,000	16,000	Eastern States.
5,000	8,000	38	17	12	80,000	100,000	2,000	2,300	Tennessee.
18,000	20,000	31	60	50	100,000	125,000	6,800	9,000	Ohio and Tennessee.
5,200	6,560	18	39	43	27,000	34,000	252	548	Tenn.,Virginia & N. Carolina.
14,400	15,900	12	10	12	400,000	500,000	6,800	10,000	N.York, S. Carolina and Tenn.
10,000	12,000	142	200	250	75,000	100,000	500	1,000	Penn.. Ky. and No. Illinois.
10,000	14,000	30	68	100	200,000	500,000	4,000	9,000	N. Y.,No. Ill. and So. States
6,000	7,000	10	20	30	60,000	130,000	2,000	3,500	Kentucky.
15,000	20,000	47	50	121	40,000	82,000	1,200	2,300	N.C.,Tenn.,N.Y.,Wis. & N.Ill.
26,000	31,000	118	24	17	65,000	200,000	1,700	3,000	Tennessee.
12,000	15,000	26	20	20	80,000	120,000	1,000	1,200	North Carolina.
2,500	3,000	49	25	12	45,000	60,000	1,800	2,000	North Carolina.
2,000	4,000	52	2	5	200	3,000	100	325	Penn., Maine and New York.
5,000	6,000	15	11	15	45,000	55,400	5,200	6,000	Vermont, N Y. and So. States.
6,000	7,000	18	0	9	140,000	160,000	750	900	New England. Ireland.
							1,300	5,200	1-3 Irish, 1-3 German and balance from all parts of U. S.
802,200	1,052,940				35,223,200	89,066,200			

Galena shipped in 1856, 190,770 pigs Lead, valued at $802,954. In 1858, 265,924 pigs, valued at $1,115,200.

Stock raising is rapidly rising in value and importance, and the attention of farmers is becoming very generally directed to it.

About 19,000,000 of acres are embraced in the territories given in the returns, though a portion of the traffic arising from the cultivation, is directed to the East and West Railroads which cross the Illinois Central.

ABSTRACT OF TITLE TO THE

Illinois Central Railroad Lands.

The lands offered for sale by the Illinois Central Railroad Company were granted by the United States to the State of Illinois, by the Act of 20th September, 1850. All the conditions stipulated in that Act have been fulfilled, and the title to these lands can no longer be affected by legislation.

By the Act of 10th February, 1851, the State of Illinois incorporated this Company, and directed the Governor to convey to said Company, by a deed in fee simple, all of said lands, etc., which was done.

The said Act further required said Company to execute a Deed of Trust of all said lands, etc., to certain persons named therein by the State, to secure the performance of the conditions and stipulations required thereby. The bonds issued under this trust are being paid as fast as the money is received from the sale of the lands set apart for that purpose. All bonds, purchased with the proceeds of such lands, are officially canceled by the Trustees.

Where payment is made in full, the purchaser at once obtains his title from the Trustees appointed by the State. If the sale is on credit, however, the title is not given till final payment is made, but the purchaser receives a Contract, stipulating that such title will be given on full payment, and compliance with the conditions specified therein. The moneys received for the sale of lands are applied to the purchase of Bonds, and the particular tract is at once exempted from liability, and a perfect title given by the Trustees—*being in fact, the first conveyance under the authority of the General Government.*

The sales are made under the sanction of the Trustees, and are authorized by an Act of the State Legislature. The lands thus sold are exempted from taxation by said law of the State till finally paid for.

The Trustees execute Deeds for all lands sold; and the conveyance by said Trustees, in the terms of the law, is *"an absolute title in fee simple,"* and operates *"as a release or an acquittance of the particular tract or tracts so sold from all liability or encumbrance on account of said Deed of Trust, and the issue of said Bonds—so as to vest in the purchasers a complete and indefeasible title."*

Thus it is seen that the Act of Congress making the grant secures the title in purchasers, whatever may be the action of the State; and the law of the State incorporating this Company, while amply securing the Bondholders, is alike careful to protect purchasers of the lands, and to secure to them perfect and complete titles in any and every contingency.

No assignment by this Company can, in the slightest degree, affect the titles of those who have purchased or may purchase any of these lands, as the titles to the whole of them are in the Trustees appointed by the Act of the Legislature incorporating this Company, whose duties are specifically designated, and the objects of the Trust fully and clearly set forth in that Act; and, as all subsequent transactions have been had with full notice that these lands were thus dedicated, none of those subsequent transactions can interfere with that dedication.

JOHN MOORE,
SAMUEL D. LOCKWOOD, } TRUSTEES.

CHICAGO, March 1, 1859.